CONTRIBUTORS

The Voice of Mark: *Let Them Listen*

D0288901

SCRIPTURES RETOLD BY:
Greg Garrett

COMMENTARY BY:
Matthew Paul Turner

SCHOLARLY REVIEW BY:
David B. Capes
Peter H. Davids

EDITORIAL REVIEW BY:
Chris Seay
James F. Couch, Jr.
Maleah Bell
Marilyn Duncan
Amanda Haley
Kelly Hall
Merrie Noland
Holly Perry

A SCRIPTURE PROJECT TO REDISCOVER THE STORY OF THE BIBLE

LET THEM LISTEN

The Gospel of Mark Retold by
Greg Garrett

with

Commentary by
Matthew Paul Turner

A SCRIPTURE PROJECT TO REDISCOVER THE STORY OF THE BIBLE

THOMAS NELSON
Since 1798

NASHVILLE   DALLAS   MEXICO CITY   RIO DE JANEIRO   BEIJING

The Voice of Mark: Let Them Listen
Copyright © 2008 Thomas Nelson, Inc.

© 2006, 2007, 2008 Ecclesia Bible Society
All rights reserved. No portion of this book may be reproduced, stored in a retrieval system,
or transmitted in any form or by any means—electronic, mechanical, photocopy, recording,
scanning, or other—except for brief quotations in critical reviews or articles, without the
prior written permission of the publisher.
Published in Nashville, Tennessee, by Thomas Nelson.
Thomas Nelson is a trademark of Thomas Nelson, Inc.

Published in association with Eames Literary Services, Nashville, Tennessee
Typesetting by Rainbow Graphics
Cover design by Scott Lee Designs

Printed in the United States of America
08 09 10 11 12 13 14 15—8 7 6 5 4 3 2 1

TABLE OF CONTENTS

Section Two // **Other products from** the voice // **115**

the voice.
A Scripture project to rediscover the story of the Bible

Any literary project reflects the age in which it is written. **The Voice** is created for and by a church in great transition. Throughout the body of Christ, extensive discussions are ongoing about a variety of issues including style of worship, how we separate culture from our theology, and what is essential truth. In fact, we are struggling with what is truth. At the center of this discussion is the role of Scripture. This discussion is heating up with strong words being exchanged. Instead of furthering the division over culture and theology, it is time to bring the body of Christ together again around the Bible. Thomas Nelson Publishers and Ecclesia Bible Society together are developing Scripture products that foster spiritual growth and theological exploration out of a heart for worship and mission. We have dedicated ourselves to hearing and proclaiming God's voice through this project.

Previously most Bibles and biblical reference works were produced by professional scholars writing in academic settings. **The Voice** uniquely represents collaboration among scholars, pastors, writers, musicians, poets, and other artists. The goal is to create the finest Bible products to help believers experience the joy and wonder of God's revelation. Four key words describe the vision of this project:

- holistic // considers heart, soul, and mind
- beautiful // achieves literary and artistic excellence
- sensitive // respects cultural shifts and the need for accuracy
- balanced // includes theologically diverse writers and scholars

Uniqueness of *The Voice*

About 40 different human authors are believed to have been inspired by God to write the Scriptures. **The Voice** retains the perspective of the human writers. Most English translations attempt to even out the styles of the different authors in sentence structure and vocabulary. Instead, **The Voice** distinguishes the uniqueness of each author. The heart of the project is retelling the story of the Bible in a form as fluid as modern literary works yet remaining true to the original manuscripts. First, accomplished writers create an English rendering; then, respected Bible scholars adjust the rendering to align the manuscript with the original texts. Attention is paid to the use of idioms, artistic elements, confusion of pronouns, repetition of conjunctives, modern sentence structure, and the public reading of the passage. In the process, the writer or scholar may adjust the arrangement of words or expand the phrasing to create an English equivalent.

To help the reader understand how the new rendering of a passage compares to the original manuscripts, several indicators are imbedded within the text. Italic type indicates words not directly tied to a dynamic translation of the original language. Material delineated by a screened box expands on the theme. This portion is not taken directly from the original language. To avoid the endless repetition of simple conjunctives, dialog is formatted as a screenplay. The speaker is indicated, the dialog is indented, and quotation marks are not used. This helps greatly in the public reading of Scripture. Sometimes the original text includes interruptions in the dialog to indicate attitude of the speaker or who is being spoken to. This is shown either as a stage direction immediately following the speaker's name or as part of the narrative section that immediately precedes the speaker's name. The screenplay format clearly shows who is speaking.

Throughout **The Voice,** other language devices improve readability. We follow the standard conventions used in most translations regarding textual evidence. **The Voice** is based on the earliest and best manuscripts from the original languages (Greek, Hebrew, and Aramaic). When significant variations influence a reading, we follow the publishing standard by bracketing the passage and placing a note at the bottom of the page while maintaining the traditional chapter and verse divisions. The footnotes reference quoted material and help the reader understand the translation for a particular word. Words that are borrowed from another language or words that are not common outside of the theological community (such as "baptism," "repentance," and "salvation") are translated into more common terminology. For clarity, some pronouns are replaced with their antecedents. Word order and parts of speech are sometimes altered to help the reader understand the original passage.

— Ecclesia Bible Society

ABOUT *THE VOICE* PROJECT

As retold, edited, and illustrated by a gifted team
of writers, scholars, poets, and storytellers

A New Way to Process Ideas

Chris Seay's (president of Ecclesia Bible Society) vision for *The Voice* goes back 15 years to his early attempts to teach the Bible in the narrative as the story of God. As Western culture has moved into what is now referred to as postmodernism, Chris observed that the way a new generation processes ideas and information raises obstacles to traditional methods of teaching biblical content. His desire has grown to present the Bible in ways that overcome these obstacles to people coming to faith. Instead of propositional-based thought patterns, people today are more likely to interact with events and individuals through complex observations involving emotions, cognitive processes, tactile experiences, and spiritual awareness. Much as in the parables of Jesus and in the metaphors of the prophets, narrative communication touches the whole person.

Hence, out of that early vision comes the need in a postmodern culture to present Scripture in a narrative form. The result is a retelling of the Scriptures: *The Voice*, not of words, but of meaning and experience.

The Timeless Narrative

The Voice is a fresh expression of the timeless narrative known as the Bible. Stories of God's goodness that were told to emerging generations by their grandparents and tribal leaders were recorded and assembled to form the Christian Scriptures. Too often, the passion, grit, humor, and beauty has been lost in the translation process. *The Voice* seeks to recapture what was lost.

From these early explorations by Chris and others has come *The Voice*: a Scripture project to rediscover the story of the Bible. Thomas Nelson Publishers and Ecclesia Bible Society have joined together to stimulate unique creative experiences and to develop Scripture products and resources to foster spiritual growth and theological exploration out of a heart for the mission of the church and worship of God.

Traditional Translations

Putting the Bible into the language of modern readers has too often been a painstaking process of correlating the biblical languages to the English vernacular. The Bible is filled with passages intended to inspire, captivate, and depict beauty. The old school of translation most often fails at attempts to communicate beauty, poetry, and story. *The Voice* is a collage of compelling narratives, poetry, song, truth, and wisdom. *The Voice* will call you to enter into the whole story of God with your heart, soul, and mind.

A New Retelling

One way to describe this approach is to say that it is a "soul translation," not just a "mind translation." But "translation" is not the right word. It is really the retelling of the story. The "retelling" involves translation and paraphrase, but mostly entering into the story of the Scriptures and recreating the event for our culture and time. It doesn't ignore the role of scholars, but it also values the role of writers, poets, songwriters, and artists. Instead, a team of scholars partner with a writer to blend the mood and voice of the original author with an accurate rendering of words of the text in English.

    The Voice is unique in that it represents collaboration among scholars, writers, musicians, and other artists. Its goal is to create the finest Bible products to help believers experience the joy and wonder of God's revelation. In this time of great transition within the church, we are seeking to give gifted individuals opportunities to craft a variety of products and experiences: a translation of the Scriptures, worship music, worship film festivals, biblical art, worship conferences, gatherings of creative thinkers, a Web site for individuals and churches to share biblical resources, and books derived from exploration during the Bible translation work.

    The heart of each product within *The Voice* project is the retelling of the Bible story. To accomplish the objectives of the project and to facilitate the various products envisioned within the project, the Bible text is being translated. We trust that this retelling will be a helpful contribution to a fresh engagement with Scripture. The Bible is the greatest story ever told, but it often doesn't read like it. *The Voice* brings the biblical narratives to life and reads more like a great novel than the traditional versions of the Bible that are seldom opened in contemporary culture.

Readable and Enjoyable

A careful process is being followed to assure that the spiritual, emotional, and artistic goals of the project are met. First, the retelling of the Bible has been designed to be readable and enjoyable by emphasizing the narrative nature of Scripture. Beyond simply providing a set of accurately translated individual words, phrases, and sentences, our teams were charged to render the biblical texts with sensitivity to the flow of the unfolding story. We asked them to see themselves not only as guardians of the sacred text, but also as storytellers, because we believe that the Bible has always been intended to be heard as the sacred story of the people of God. We assigned each literary unit (for example, the writings of John or Paul) to a team that included a skilled writer and biblical and theological scholars, seeking to achieve a mixture of scholarly expertise and literary skill.

Personal and Diverse

Second, as a consequence of this team approach, **The Voice** is both personal and diverse. God used about 40 human instruments to communicate His message, and each one has a unique voice or literary style. Standard translations tend to flatten these individual styles so that each book reads more or less like the others—with a kind of impersonal textbook-style prose. Some translations and paraphrases have paid more attention to literary style—but again, the literary style of one writer, no matter how gifted, can unintentionally obscure the diversity of the original voices. To address these problems, we asked our teams to try to feel and convey the diverse literary styles of the original authors.

Faithful

Third, we have taken care that **The Voice** is faithful and that it avoids prejudice. Anyone who has worked with translation and paraphrase knows that there is no such thing as a completely unbiased or objective translation. So, while we do not pretend to be purely objective, we asked our teams to seek to be as faithful as possible to the biblical message as they understood it together. In addition, as we partnered biblical scholars and theologians with our writers, we intentionally built teams that did not share any single theological tradition. Their diversity has helped each of them not to be trapped within his or her own individual preconceptions, resulting in a faithful and fresh rendering of the Bible.

Stimulating and Creative

Fourth, we have worked hard to make ***The Voice*** both stimulating and creative. As we engaged the biblical text, we realized again and again that certain terms have conventional associations for modern readers that would not have been present for the original readers—and that the original readers would have been struck by certain things that remain invisible or opaque to modern readers. Even more, we realized that modern readers from different religious or cultural traditions would hear the same words differently. For example, when Roman Catholic or Eastern Orthodox readers encounter the word "baptism," a very different set of meanings and associations come to mind than those that would arise in the minds of Baptist or Pentecostal readers. And a secular person encountering the text would have still different associations. The situation is made even more complex when we realize that *none* of these associations may resemble the ones that would have come to mind when John invited Jewish peasants and Pharisees into the water of the Jordan River in the months before Jesus began His public ministry. It is far harder than most people realize to help today's readers recapture the original impact of a single word like "baptism." In light of this challenge, we decided, whenever possible, to select words that would stimulate fresh thinking rather than reinforce unexamined assumptions. We want the next generation of Bible readers—whatever their background—to have the best opportunity possible to hear God's message the way the first generation of Bible readers heard it.

Transformative

Finally, we desire that this translation will be useful and transformative. It is all too common in many of our Protestant churches to have only a few verses of biblical text read in a service, and then that selection too often becomes a jumping-off point for a sermon that is at best peripherally related to, much less rooted in, the Bible itself. The goal of ***The Voice*** is to promote the public reading of longer sections of Scripture—followed by thoughtful engagement with the biblical narrative in its richness and fullness and dramatic flow. We believe the Bible itself, in all its diversity and energy and dynamism, is the message; it is not merely the jumping-off point.

The various creations of the project bring creative application of commentary and interpretive tools. These are clearly indicated and separated from the Bible text that is drawn directly from traditional sources. Along with the creative resources and fresh expressions of God's Word, the reader has the benefit of centuries of biblical research applied dynamically to our rapidly changing culture.

The products underway in **The Voice** include dynamic and interactive presentations of the critical passages in the life of Jesus and the early church, recorded musical presentation of Scripture originally used in worship or uniquely structured for worship, artwork commissioned from young artists, dramatized audio presentations from the Gospels and the Old Testament historical books, film commentary on our society using the words of Scripture, and exploration of the voice of each human author of the Bible.

The first product for **The Voice**, entitled *The Last Eyewitness: The Final Week*, released Spring 2006, follows Jesus through His final week of life on earth through the firsthand account of John the apostle. This book combines the drama of the text with the artwork of Rob Pepper into a captivating retelling of Jesus' final days. The second product, *The Dust Off Their Feet: Lessons from the First Church*, was released September 2006 and includes the entire Book of Acts retold by Brian McLaren with commentary and articles written by nine scholars and pastors. *The Voice of Matthew* was released January 2007 with the Gospel of Matthew retold by Lauren Winner including Lauren's devotional commentary, along with cultural and historical notes. *The Voice of Luke: Not Even Sandals*, released June 2007, contains the Gospel of Luke retold by Brian McLaren and includes his devotional notes.

The Voice from on High, published in the fall of 2007, contains over 700 verses from 19 Old Testament and New Testament books. The story of the Liberating King is shown to run through the Bible from Genesis to Revelation. Over a dozen writers have contributed to the retelling of the Scriptures with reflections by Jonathan Hal Reynolds. *The Voice Revealed*, also published in the fall of 2007, is the full Gospel of John retold by Chris Seay in a compact edition to introduce others to the faith.

The Voice of Hebrews: The Mystery of Melchizedek, released February, 2008, combines the Book of Hebrews retold by Greg Garrett with commentary by David B. Capes. This retelling helps readers understand how Jesus completes the law and prophets and compares the character from Genesis, Melchizedek, and the Liberator, Jesus. The next book, *The Voice of Romans,* will be published in the summer of 2008.

The Team

The team writing **The Voice** brings unprecedented gifts to this unique project. An award-winning fiction writer, an acclaimed poet, a pastor renowned for using art and narrative in his preaching and teaching, Greek and Hebrew authorities, and biblical scholars are all coming together to capture the beauty and diversity of God's Word.

Writers

The contributors to *The Voice of Mark: Let Them Listen* are:

- Greg Garrett—Professor of English at Baylor University and writer in residence at the Episcopal Theological Seminary of the Southwest. He is the author of the critically acclaimed novels *Free Bird* and *Cycling*, the memoir *Crossing Myself*, and nonfiction books, including *The Gospel Reloaded* (with Chris Seay) and *The Gospel According to Hollywood*.

- Matthew Paul Turner—Former editor of *CCM* magazine. He is the author of *The Christian Culture Survival Guide*, *Provocative Faith*, and the memoir *Churched*. With a focus on sharing spiritual relevancy in today's culture, Matthew is a frequent speaker at college and twenty-something events across the country.

along with

- David B. Capes, PhD—Professor of Greek and New Testament at Houston Baptist University. He has written several books, including *The Last Eyewitness: the Final Week, Rediscovering Paul,* and *The Footsteps of Jesus in the Holy Land*.

- Peter H. Davids, PhD—Adjunct Professor at Tyndale Theological Amsterdam, International Teams Innsbrook, and resident scholar at Basileia Vineyard Bern. He is the author of commentaries on the books of James, 1 & 2 Peter, and Jude and is the editor of the *Dictionary of Late New Testament and Its Development*.

The writers for **The Voice** include:

Isaac Anderson—writer/musician
Eric Bryant—pastor/author
David B. Capes—professor/author

Don Chaffer—singer/songwriter/poet
Lori Chaffer—singer/songwriter/poet
Tara Leigh Cobble—singer/songwriter
Robert Creech—pastor/author
Greg Garrett—professor/author
Christena Graves—singer
Sara Groves—singer/songwriter
Amanda Haley—archaeology scholar/editor
Charlie Hall—singer/songwriter
Kelly Hall—editor/poet
Greg Holder—pastor
Justin Hyde—pastor/author
Andrew Jones—pastor/consultant
E. Chad Karger—counselor/author/pastor
Tim Keel—pastor
Greg LaFollette—musician/songwriter
Evan Lauer—pastor/author
Phuc Luu—chaplain/adjunct instructor
Christian McCabe—pastor/artist
Brian McLaren—pastor/author
Donald Miller—author
Sean Palmer—pastor
Jonathan Hal Reynolds—poet
Chris Seay—pastor/author
Robbie Seay—singer/songwriter
Kerry Shook—pastor
Chuck Smith, Jr.—pastor/author
Allison Smythe—poet
Leonard Sweet—author
Kristin Swenson—professor/author
Alison Thomas—speaker/apologist
Phyllis Tickle—author
Matthew Paul Turner—author/speaker
Lauren Winner—lecturer/author
Seth Woods—singer/songwriter
Dieter Zander—pastor/author

Scholars

Biblical and theological scholars for **The Voice** include:

Joseph Blair, ThD—professor
Darrell L. Bock, PhD—professor
David B. Capes, PhD—author/professor, HBU
Alan Culpepper, PhD—dean/professor
Peter H. Davids, PhD—pastor/professor
J. Andrew Dearman, PhD—professor
J. R. Dodson, MDiv—adjunct professor
Brett Dutton, PhD—pastor/adjunct professor
Dave Garber, PhD—professor
Mark Gignilliat, PhD—assistant professor
Peter Rhea Jones, Sr., PhD—pastor/professor
Sheri Klouda, PhD—professor
Tremper Longman, PhD—professor
Creig Marlowe, PhD—dean/professor
Troy Miller, PhD—professor
Frank Patrick—assistant professor
Chuck Pitts, PhD—professor
Brian Russell, PhD—associate professor
Nancy de Claissé Walford, PhD—professor
Kenneth Waters, Sr., PhD—professor
Jack Wisdom, JD—lawyer

A WORD ABOUT THIS BOOK ...

Each of the four Gospels is unique. The literary style, audience, and the perspective of the writer differ in large and small ways. The Gospel of Mark holds a unique place. It is as though Mark is writing to the kind of person I seem to encounter on a daily basis, the kind of person who says, "Don't tell me what you believe—I don't really care. I want to see how you live, the way you treat people, what your spirituality looks like, and what you do with your time."

In Mark's Gospel, you discover what Jesus is about by watching what He does. Almost anyone can talk the talk. But if Jesus really is the Liberating King, the readers of this Gospel want to see Him liberate. You will have to judge for yourself how Jesus loves, heals, and liberates. But I can assure you that Mark is giving you the straight scoop on what Jesus did.

So that you could experience the story with the rich tone and fervor of Mark, we chose the most gifted fiction writer we know. Greg Garrett is a novelist, winner of the William Faulkner Prize for Fiction, a teacher, a lover of Jesus, and a dear friend. He retells this narrative with a skill that will allow you to get lost in the story of Jesus. Greg collaborated with numerous scholars, including Peter Davids and my friend David Capes; and ultimately, we were blessed to add the unique perspective of Matthew Paul Turner, a fabulous writer, humorous speaker, and activist.

So pick up this book, and gaze well into the life of Jesus. It will change the way you live!

Blessings,
Chris Seay
President, Ecclesia Bible Society

Section One // **The Gospel of Mark**

Introduction

The Gospel of Mark may be compared to an action-packed movie. That does indeed make this Gospel sound a little hip; and truthfully, that analogy is not incorrect. Throughout John Mark's retelling of Jesus' story, there are indeed many Hollywood-esque themes—some that keep us on the edge of our seats, some that make us cry, and some that leave us in wonderment.

Like the author of a controversial and provocative film that's been made primarily to awaken audiences to truth, the writer of the second Gospel wastes no time on frills; he immediately engages the readers by introducing them to the drama, tension, characterization, and truth about Jesus. He skips the fluff of trying to describe the emotions of Jesus and His followers, and he gets right to business telling the story of what Jesus actually does. You ought to know that Jesus does not disappoint; He performs signs before breakfast that defy explanation, and He offers hope that all can be rescued from the most horrific trials.

The Gospel according to Mark stands out among the books of the Bible that chronicle the life of Jesus. Unlike the detailed characters and conversations that we encounter in the words of Luke or Matthew, or the unique personal account in John's Gospel, Mark's story about Jesus is colored by his passion and excitement for the stories he writes. Just as the smile on a man's face reveals the love and excitement he feels for his bride, Mark's fast-paced prose continuously exposes how eager he is to make Jesus known. Mark writes like a man on a mission. And maybe that's what's driving him—a mission to help everyone hear the story about the Liberating King, Jesus! As the first to write down Jesus' story, Mark tells it quickly; he focuses on the highlights and hurries to get to the best part, which for him, is the story's climax.

When Mark writes in the first chapter about a mysterious man entering the scene, instantly you know there's something very different about Him. He comes into the picture not as a rock star but rather as someone humble, kind, and yet, still kingly. Soon after we meet the protagonist of the story, Mark begins sharing about the people who are drawn toward this man— regular people like you and me who have become affected by the character, passion, and light of this strange Galilean.

Maybe that's why Mark jumps right into the action of Jesus' story. He offers little by way of introduction. He writes nothing about Jesus' family tree.

Unlike Matthew and Luke, he doesn't mention His birth. Mark's retelling begins with Scripture and the preaching of John, the wandering prophet. Like all the greats of history, Jesus doesn't just arrive; He is announced, and who better than John to do that? Right before Jesus makes His entrance into Mark's narrative, John says, "I've washed you here with water, *but when He gets here*, He will wash you in the Spirit of God."

PREPARE THE WAY

¹This is the beginning of the good news of Jesus the Liberating King, the Son of God.

²Isaiah the prophet told us *what would happen before the Liberator came when he delivered the words of God:*

> "Watch, I will send My messenger in front of You
>> to prepare Your way and make it clear *and straight.**
> ³*You'll hear him,* a voice crying in the wilderness,
>> 'Prepare the way of the Eternal One,
>>> a straight way in the wandering desert, a highway for our
>>> God.'"*

⁴*That messenger was* John the Prophet,* who appeared in the desert *near the Jordan River* preaching that people should be ritually cleansed* *with water as a sign of* both their changed hearts* and God's forgiveness of their sins. ⁵People from across the countryside of Judea and from the city of Jerusalem came to him and confessed that they were deeply flawed and needed help, so he cleansed* them with the waters of the Jordan.

1:2 Malachi 3:1
1:3 Isaiah 40:3
1:4 Literally, John who immersed to show repentance
1:4 Literally, immersed, to show repentance
1:4 Literally, repentance
1:5 Literally, immersed, to show repentance

According to Luke's Gospel, John was the only child of a Jewish priest named Zacharias and his wife Elizabeth, who was a cousin to Mary, the mother of Jesus. Zacharias and Elizabeth didn't think they could have children, so when Elizabeth became pregnant with John very late in life, it was quite surprising. In fact, Zacharias doubted; he didn't believe his wife could bear a child. Then one day Gabriel, the messenger of the Lord, visited him at the temple. The heavenly messenger not only announced John's birth, but also told Zacharias what the baby should be named and what his role in the Liberating King's story would be. However, because of Zacharias's unbelief, he lost his ability to speak until the day of John's circumcision—six months prior to Jesus' birth.

6John dressed *as some of the Hebrew prophets had,* in clothes made of camels' hair with a leather belt around his waist. He made his meals *in the desert* from locusts and wild honey. 7He preached a message *in the wilderness.*

John the Prophet | Someone is coming who is a lot more powerful than I am—One whose sandals I'm not worthy to bend down and untie. 8I've washed* you here with water; *but when He gets here,* He will wash* you in the Spirit of God.

1:8 Literally, immersed, to show repentance
1:8 Literally, immerse, in a rite of initiation and purification

*T*he Jordan River is the setting of some of the most memorable miracles in the First Testament. On their journey through the wilderness to the promised land, the Israelites walked across the Jordan River on dry ground because God parted its waters. Elisha, one of the prophets of God, healed Naaman by telling him to bathe seven times in its waters. Partly because of miracles like these and partly because of a growing wilderness spirituality, many of the Jews in John's day went out to hear him and be dipped in its cool, cleansing waters. They were looking for God to intervene miraculously in their lives as He had done in the past. What they didn't know was that God was about to intervene for, at that time, Jesus left Nazareth and headed south.

⁹It was in those days that Jesus left Nazareth (*a village in the region* of Galilee) and came down to the Jordan, and John cleansed* Him there *in the same way all the others were ritually cleansed.* ¹⁰But as Jesus was coming out of the waters, He looked up and saw the sky split open. The Spirit *of God* descended upon Him like a dove, ¹¹and a voice echoed in the heavens.

> **Voice** | You are My Son, My beloved One, and I am very pleased with You.*

¹²After that the Spirit compelled Him to go into the wilderness, ¹³and there in the desert He stayed for 40 days. He was tested by

---

1:9 Literally, immersed
1:11 Psalm 2:7

Satan himself and surrounded by wild animals; *but through these trials,* heavenly messengers *cared for Him and* ministered to Him.

¹⁴After John was arrested *by Herod, who ruled the Jewish lands on behalf of Roman interests,* Jesus went back into *the region of* Galilee and began to proclaim the good news of God.

> Jesus | ¹⁵It's time! The kingdom of God is near! Seek forgiveness, change your actions,* and believe this good news!

¹⁶As Jesus walked along the *shore of the* Sea of Galilee, He met *the first of His disciples,* two brothers, Simon and Andrew, both fishermen, who were casting their fishing net into the shallow waters.

> Jesus | ¹⁷*Come and* follow Me, and I'll send you to catch people *instead of fish.*

¹⁸Simon and Andrew left their nets and followed Jesus at once.

¹⁹When He had walked a little farther, He saw the sons of Zebedee, James and John, in their boat repairing their nets. ²⁰Right away He called to them, and they dropped what they were doing and left their father Zebedee and the hired men aboard the boat to follow Him *as His disciples.*

²¹They came *at last* to the village of Capernaum *on the Sea of Galilee*; and on the Sabbath Day, Jesus went straight into a synagogue, *sat down,* and began to teach. ²²The people *looked at each other,* amazed, because this strange teacher acted as One authorized *by God, and what He taught affected them* in ways their own scribes' teachings could not.

1:15 Literally, repent

*J*esus was no stranger to the synagogue; His parents were faithful Jewish folk who taught their children the traditions of their faith. When He was twelve years old, His parents took Him to Jerusalem for the Passover celebration. When the family made the trip home, Jesus' parents realized He wasn't with them; so they returned to Jerusalem to find Him sitting with the Jewish teachers, teaching them about God. Here, we read about Jesus teaching at the synagogue as an adult.

[23]Just then, a man in the gathering who was overcome by an unclean spirit shouted.

Unclean Spirit | [24]What are You doing here, Jesus of Nazareth? Have You come to destroy us? I can see who You are! You're the Holy One of God.

Jesus | [25]Be quiet, and come out of him now!
(*rebuking him*)

[26]The man's body began to shake and shudder; and then, howling, the spirit flew out of the man. [27]The people couldn't stop talking about what they had seen.

People | *Who is this Jesus?* This is a new teaching—and it has such authority! Even the unclean spirits obey His commands!

²⁸It wasn't long before news of Jesus spread over the countryside of Galilee.

²⁹Right after they left the synagogue, Jesus went with James and John to the home of Simon and Andrew. ³⁰They told Him about Simon's mother-in-law who was there in bed, sick and feverish. ³¹Jesus went to her side, took her hand, and lifted her up. As soon as He touched her, the fever left her *and she felt well again—strong enough to bustle around the house* taking care of her visitors.

³²Just before night fell, others had gathered all the sick, *diseased,* and demon-infested people *they could find.* ³³*It seemed as if* the whole town had gathered at Simon and Andrew's door. ³⁴Jesus was kept busy healing people of every sort of ailment and casting out unclean spirits. He was very careful not to let the demons speak because they knew Him *and could reveal to the people who He really was.*

³⁵Early in the morning, Jesus got up, left the house while it was still dark outside, and went to a deserted place to pray. ³⁶Simon and the others traveling with Jesus looked for Him. ³⁷They finally tracked Him down.

*W*henever possible, Jesus sought out solitude so He could pray and meditate. Perhaps this was just one of the ways Jesus revealed His humanity. In these silent and reflective moments, He seemed to refuel mentally, physically, and spiritually because Jesus heard His Father speak during His time alone. Throughout Jesus' ministry on earth, hearing from His Father seemed to help Him focus on the mission at hand: redemption.

People | Everybody wants to know where You are!

Jesus | ³⁸It's time we went somewhere else—the next vil-
lage, maybe—so I can tell more people *the good news
about the kingdom of God.* After all, that's the reason
I'm here.

³⁹So He traveled *to the next village and the one after that,* throughout the
region of Galilee, teaching in the synagogues and casting out unclean spirits *as His students trailed along and watched.*
⁴⁰*During that time, Jesus met a man stricken with leprosy—a skin disease
that many people thought made him ritually unclean.* The leper walked
right up to Jesus, dropped to his knees, and begged Him for help.

Leper | If You want to, You can make me clean.

⁴¹Jesus was powerfully moved. He reached out and actually touched
the leper.

Jesus | I do want to. Be clean.

⁴²And at that very moment the disease left him; the leper was
cleansed *and made whole once again.* ⁴³Jesus sent him away, but first He
warned him strongly.

Jesus | ⁴⁴Don't tell anybody how this happened. Just go and
show yourself to the priest, *so that he can certify
you're clean.* Perform the ceremony prescribed by
Moses as proof of your cleansing, *and then you may
return home.*

⁴⁵*But, of course, good news is hard to keep quiet.* The man talked everywhere about how Jesus had healed him, until Jesus could no longer come into a town openly *without the risk of being mobbed.* So He remained on the outskirts. Even so, people still sought Him out from far and wide.

LORD OVER THE SABBATH

1-2Some days later when Jesus came back to Capernaum, people heard that Jesus was back in town and many gathered at the house where He was staying. Soon, the crowd overflowed from the house into the streets, *and still more people pressed forward* to hear Jesus teaching the message *of God's kingdom.* 3Four men tried to bring a crippled friend to Him; 4but since the crowd prevented their carrying him close enough to get Jesus' attention, they climbed up onto the roof, opened a hole in it, and lowered the paralyzed man on his mat down to Jesus.

5Jesus recognized the faith of these men.

Jesus *(to the paralyzed man)*	Son, your sins are forgiven.

6Some scribes were sitting in the crowd, *and they didn't like what they were hearing.*

Scribes *(reasoning to themselves)*	6-7What does this Jesus think He is doing? This kind of talk is blasphemy, *an offense against the Most High!* Only God can forgive sins.

8At once, Jesus realized what they were thinking. He turned to them.

Jesus	Why do My words trouble you so? 9*Think about this:* is it easier to tell this paralyzed man, "Your sins are

forgiven," or to tell him, "Get up, pick up your mat, and walk"? [10]Still, I want to show you that the Son of Man has been given the authority on earth to forgive sins.

  (to the paralytic) [11]Get up, pick up your mat, and go home.

[12]The man rose to his feet, immediately rolled up his mat, and walked out *into the streets*. Everyone in the crowd was amazed. All they could do was *shake their heads,* thank God for this miracle, and say to each other, "We've never seen anything like that!"

*T*o some who believed wholeheartedly in God's laws, Jesus was a troublemaker, a mere man who had a bad habit of making statements that took away from the honor due to the one, true God. The "scribes" who made these kinds of accusations against Jesus were usually connected to the Pharisees (a Jewish sect popular with the people, mostly middle-class, and religiously strict when it came to following God's laws) or the Sadducees (a smaller Jewish sect made up of priests and aristocrats from Jerusalem). While the two groups often clashed with each other politically and theologically, they did find common ground—and sometimes even worked to-gether—in opposing Jesus.

[13]Another time, Jesus was out walking alongside the Sea *of Galilee* teaching the gathering crowd as He went. [14]He saw Levi, the son of Alphaeus, sitting at the booth where he collected taxes.

Jesus | Follow Me.
(calling out to him) |

Levi left the booth and went along with Him.

> *J*esus' invitation to follow Him, like His invitations to all the
> disciples, involved a lot more than joining the caravan; Jesus' invita-
> tion was for sinners to change their way of life. Jesus makes it clear,
> despite the criticisms of some observers, that this invitation is indeed
> open to all—especially to the sinners who need it most. Jesus grants
> to those who choose Him not just companionship and forgiveness,
> but the ability to truly receive a new identity and live a new life.

¹⁵At Levi's house, many tax collectors and other sinners—*Jews who
did not keep the strict purity laws of the Jewish holy texts*—were dining
with Jesus and His disciples. Jesus had attracted such a large following that all kinds of people surrounded Him. ¹⁶When the Pharisees'
scribes saw who shared the table with Jesus, they were quick to criti-
cize:

Scribes | *If your master is such a righteous person,* then why
(to His disciples) | does He eat and drink with tax collectors and sin-
ners, *the worst among us?*

¹⁷Jesus heard them.

Jesus | People who have their health don't need to see a
(to the scribes) | doctor. Only those who are sick do. I'm not here to

call those already in good standing with God; I'm here to call sinners to turn back to Him.

[18]The disciples of John *the Prophet* and the Pharisees made a practice of fasting.

*I*t was common for religious Jews to fast twice a week and pray three times daily, but Jesus would have a different set of practices for His followers. Since many believed that conformity to these traditions was the measure of holiness, some of the pious were disturbed by the actions, or we might say the inaction, of Jesus and His disciples.

Some People | Why is it that John's followers and the Pharisees'
(to Jesus) | followers fast, but Your disciples are eating and drinking *like it was any other day*?

Jesus | [19]Guests at the wedding can't fast when the bridegroom is with them. It would be wrong to do anything but feast. [20]When the bridegroom is snatched away from them, then the time will come to fast *and mourn.*

[21]*These are new things I'm teaching, and they can't be reconciled with old habits.* Nobody would ever use a piece of new cloth to patch an old garment because when the patch shrinks, it pulls away and makes the tear even worse. [22]And nobody puts new, *unfermented*

wine into old wineskins because if he does, the wine will burst the skins; they would lose both the wineskins and the wine. No, the only appropriate thing is to put new wine into new wineskins.

²³One Sabbath, Jesus and His disciples were walking through a field of grain; and as they walked, His disciples *grew hungry*. They began to pull from the stalks *and eat*

²⁴The Pharisees *saw a chance to attack Jesus because of the actions of His followers, so they* confronted Him.

> **Pharisees** | Did You see that? Why are Your disciples doing what our law forbids on the Sabbath?

> **Jesus** | ²⁵Do you remember the story about what *King*
> *(turning toward*
> *the Pharisees)* | David and his followers did when they were hungry and had nothing to eat?

They said nothing, so He continued.

> **Jesus** | ²⁶David went into the house of God, when Abiathar was the high priest, and ate the bread that was consecrated to God. Now our laws say no one but the priests can eat that holy bread; *but when David was hungry, he ate* and also shared the bread with those who followed him.
> ²⁷The Sabbath was made for *the needs of* human beings, and not the other way around. ²⁸So the Son of Man is Lord even over the Sabbath.

Mark 3

Jesus' True Family

¹*Soon, the Pharisees had another chance to confront Jesus. On the Sabbath,* Jesus had come into a synagogue where He saw a man with a withered hand.

²The Pharisees held their breath: would Jesus cure this man on the Sabbath, *right there in front of everyone*? If so, they could charge Him *with breaking the Sabbath law.* ³*Jesus knew their hearts.* He called to the man with the withered hand.

Jesus | Come to Me.

⁴Then He turned to the Pharisees with a question.

Jesus | Do our laws tell us to do good or evil on the Sabbath? To save life, or to snuff it out?

They remained silent.

⁵Jesus was furious as He looked out over the crowd, and He was grieved by their hard hearts. *How could anyone care so much about the words of the law and so little about the spirit of it?*

Jesus
(to the man with the withered hand) | *So be it.* Stretch out your hand.

The man stretched forth his hand; and as he did, it was completely healed. ⁶The Pharisees *didn't say anything to Jesus, but their actions spoke loudly. They* went directly from the synagogue to consult with the supporters of Herod, *the Romans' puppet ruler,* about how they could get rid of this dangerous dreamer.

⁷Meanwhile, Jesus and His followers traveled to *the shore of* the Sea *of Galilee; and as always,* a huge crowd from Galilee and Judea gathered. ⁸People had come *from miles* to see this man they were hearing so much about. They came from *the big cities, including* Jerusalem *of Judea,* Tyre and Sidon *of Phoenicia,* and from the region of Idumea, south of Judea. ⁹⁻¹⁰Since Jesus had healed so many, the sick and the infirm pushed forward constantly to touch Him, *to be healed, and to ask His blessing.* The crowd pressed so closely around Jesus that He asked His disciples to get a boat He could board if the crush became too great.

¹¹*Everyone wanted to be near Him, except for those possessed by* unclean spirits. Those people fell down before Him.

Unclean Spirits	You are the Son of God.

¹²But He ordered them not to reveal His true identity.

¹³Jesus called together a select group *of His followers* and led them up onto a mountain. ¹⁴There He commissioned them the twelve [*later,* He calls them His emissaries].* He wanted them to be with Him. He sent them out to spread the good news ¹⁵and to cast out evil spirits [and heal diseases].* ¹⁶Here are the names of the original twelve: Simon (whom Jesus called Peter, *meaning "the rock"*), ¹⁷James and John (the sons of Zebedee, whom Jesus called "the Sons of Thunder"), ¹⁸Andrew, Philip, Bartholomew, Matthew *(the tax collector,*

3:14 Most manuscripts omit this portion.
3:15 Most manuscripts omit this portion.

also called Levi), Thomas, James (the son of Alphaeus), Thaddaeus, Simon of Canaan (who was also called "the Zealot"), ¹⁹and Judas Iscariot (who one day would betray Jesus *to the authorities in Jerusalem so God's purpose could be fulfilled*).

²⁰Jesus *and His disciples* went into a house to eat, but so many people pressed in to see Jesus that they could not be served. ²¹When Jesus' family heard *about this craziness*, they went to drag Him out of that place.

Jesus' Family *(to one another)*	*This is dangerous.* Jesus has lost His mind.

²²The scribes, *for their part,* came down from Jerusalem *and spread the slander that Jesus was in league with the devil.*

Scribes	That's how He casts out demons. He's casting them out by the power of Beelzebul—*the ancient Philistine god*—the prince of demons.

²³When Jesus heard this, He tried to reason with them using parables.

Jesus	*Listen.* How can Satan drive out Satan? *Darkness drive out darkness?* ²⁴A kingdom that makes war against itself will collapse. ²⁵A household divided against itself cannot stand. ²⁶If Satan opposes himself, he cannot stand and is finished. ²⁷If you want to break into the house of a strong man and plunder it, you have to bind him first. Then you can do whatever you want with his

possessions. [28] Listen, the truth is that people can be forgiven of almost anything. *God forgives all sorts of nonsense,* any kind of blasphemy. [29]But speaking evil of the Spirit of God is an unforgivable sin that will follow you into eternity.

[30]He said this because the scribes were telling people that Jesus got His power from dark forces instead of from God.

*P*opularity is often a dangerous thing, particularly in a land occupied by Roman soldiers. As Jesus' ministry grew, some of His friends and family started to get nervous: They wondered if He had "lost His mind" entirely. Surrounded by crowds wanting to hear His teaching and to experience His healing touch, His family just couldn't understand what was happening and why He was so important. It must not have seemed right—the kid from Nazareth setting Himself up like that. In fact, they were so uncomfortable with it that they decided to intervene and take Him home.

But Jesus' family wasn't the only group trying to undermine Him. The Pharisees were doing their best to spread doubt about His authority with the worst accusations possible: His power to heal came from the devil himself. When the Pharisees accused Him of getting His power from demonic sources, they were attacking Him publicly and questioning His identity as the Liberating King.

[31]When Jesus' mother and brothers arrived, *they couldn't break through the crowd,* so they sent word in to Jesus that He should come out to

them. ³²The crowd was pressed in tight around Him when He received the message, "Your mother and brothers [and sisters]* are waiting outside for You."

³³*Jesus looked around.*

Jesus | Who are My mother and brothers?
(answering them)

He called into the silence. No one spoke.

³⁴At last, His gaze swept across those gathered close, *and Jesus smiled.*

Jesus | You, here, are My mother and My brothers!
³⁵Whoever does the will of God is My true family, *a family that's formed not of blood but of spirit. You are My family.*

3:32 Some manuscripts omit this portion.

PUZZLED BY PARABLES

¹⁻²Jesus went out again to teach by the Sea *of Galilee*; and when the crowd became unmanageable, He climbed aboard a boat and sat down to teach the people listening on the shore by telling them parables. One of His teachings went like this:

> **Jesus |** ³Listen! A farmer went out and sowed his seed, *broadcasting it left and right out of a pouch he wore around his neck.* ⁴As he scattered it, one seed fell along the *hardened* path, and a bird flapped down and snapped it up. ⁵One seed fell onto rocky places where the soil was thin, so it sprang up quickly. ⁶But when the hot sun scorched *the fragile stems and leaves,* the seedling withered because its roots didn't go deep in the soil. ⁷One of the seeds fell among the *weeds and* thorns, which crowded the seedling out of producing a crop. ⁸And the rest of the seeds fell in good, rich soil. When they sprouted, the plants grew and produced 30, 60, even 100 seeds for every one that the farmer had sown.
>
> ⁹All who have ears to hear, let them listen.

¹⁰When they were alone, the twelve and others close to Him asked why He always taught in parables *instead of explaining His teachings clearly.*

Jesus | ¹¹God has let you in on the inside story regarding the workings of the Kingdom—the hidden meanings. But the crowds—I teach them in parables ¹²*as the prophet Isaiah predicted,*

> So that when they look, they see and yet do not understand.
> When they hear, they listen and yet do not comprehend.
> Otherwise, they might really turn and be forgiven.*

*his made the disciples scratch their heads. They themselves were already puzzled by the parables. Why would He want to hide the truth from some people? His teachings were hard enough without putting them into parables.

Jesus | ¹³Do you mean to say that you didn't understand My parable of the sower? *That was the key parable. If you don't see what I was trying to teach there,* how will you be able to understand any of the others?

¹⁴The seed the farmer is sowing is *the good news,* God's word. ¹⁵Some people are the seed thrown onto the path, and the tempter snaps up the word *before it can even take root.* ¹⁶Others are the seed thrown among the rocks. Those people hear the

---

4:12 Isaiah 6:9-10

word and receive it immediately with joy and enthusiasm; [17]but without deep roots, *doubt,* trouble, or persecution instantly withers their faith. [18]Still others are the seed tossed among *weeds and brambles.* The word has reached them, [19]but the things of this life—the worries, the drive for more and more, the desire for other things—those things *cluster around close and* choke the life of God out of them until they cannot produce. [20]But those last seeds—those sown into good soil? Those people hear the word, accept it, *meditate on it, act on it,* and bear fruit—a crop 30, 60, or 100 times larger *than the farmer dropped to earth.*

*J*esus' teaching often included parables: stories that explain the truth about the Kingdom with examples from the everyday lives of His hearers. Considering that most of His listeners knew about farming, it's no wonder that most of Jesus' parables were based on agricultural realities: sowing seeds, pruning weeds, harvesting crops. The farmers in His audience that day would have had no trouble picturing this story as He described it; it was something they did every season. They had seen firsthand the birds landing in the field gobbling up their seed. They had seen how some seed sprang up on the rocky edges of the field only to have them bake in the hot sun. They had seen how weeds choked out the tender seedlings and produced nothing. But—and this was the good news—they knew that most of their seed fell into good, rockless, weed-free soil and produced a crop that would feed them and their families this year and the next.

Parables like this forced Jesus' listeners to think about the reality of the kingdom of God differently. He challenged their ideas and wishes for the future. As a master teacher, He also knew that they were unlikely to forget it. Every season when they saw farmers broadcasting their seeds, they would remember this parable and ponder the mysteries of the Kingdom just as Jesus wanted. It never seemed to bother Him that people were confused by His teaching. He didn't expect them to understand everything; He didn't even want them to. Instead, He wanted them to wrestle with His teachings so His words would sit in their hearts and simmer—much like the seed sitting in good soil that eventually grows to bear fruit.

Jesus | ²¹When you bring a lamp *into the house,* do you put it under a box or *stuff it* under your bed? Or do you set it on top of a table *or chest*? ²²Those things that are hidden are meant to be revealed, and what is concealed is meant to be brought out where its light can shine.

²³All who have ears to hear, let them listen.

²⁴*That's why I do what I do.* So consider carefully the things you're hearing. If you put it to use, you'll be given more to wrestle with—much more. ²⁵Those who have *listened* will receive more, but those who don't hear will forget even the little they've failed to understand.

²⁶Here is what the kingdom of God is like: a man who throws seeds onto the earth. ²⁷Day and night, as he works and as he sleeps, the seeds

sprout and climb out into the light, even though he doesn't understand how it works. ²⁸*It's as though* the soil itself produced the grain *somehow*—from a sprouted stalk to ripened fruit. ²⁹But *however it happens,* when he sees that the grain has grown and ripened, he gets his sickle and begins to cut it because the harvest has come.

³⁰What else is the kingdom of God like? What earthly thing can we compare it to? ³¹The kingdom of God is like a mustard seed, the tiniest seed you can sow. ³²But after that seed is planted, it grows into the largest plant in the garden, a plant so big that birds can build their nests in the shade of its branches.

³³Jesus spoke many parables like these to the people who followed Him. ³⁴This was the only way He taught them, although when He was alone with His chosen few, He interpreted all the stories *so the disciples truly understood.*

³⁵The same evening, Jesus suggested they cross over to the other side *of the lake.* ³⁶With Jesus already in the boat, they left the crowd behind and set sail along with a few other boats that followed. ³⁷*As they sailed,* a storm formed; and *the winds whipped up* huge waves that broke over the bow, filling the boat *with so much water that even the experienced sailors among them were sure they were going to sink.*

³⁸Jesus was back in the stern of the boat, sound asleep on a cushion, when the disciples shook Him awake.

| Disciples (shouting over the storm) | Jesus, Master, don't You care that we're going to die? |

³⁹He got up, shouted words into the wind, and commanded the waves.

> **Jesus** | That's enough! Be still!

And immediately the wind died down to nothing, the waves stopped, *and the surface of the sea was as smooth as a sheet of glass.*

> **Jesus** | ⁴⁰How can you be so afraid? *After all you've seen,*
>   where is your faith?

⁴¹The disciples were still afraid, *looking about them in every direction, slowly coming to grips with what they had seen.*

> **Disciples** | Who is this *Jesus*? How can it be that He has power
> *(to one another)* | over even the wind and the waves?

For most of Jesus' miracles, the disciples were observers: they watched Him heal the sick, raise dead bodies, and cast demons out of strangers. But they were merely watching, there to record the events instead of being part of them. This time, however, it was the disciples—and even Jesus Himself—who were in danger; and maybe that's why they had such a hard time trusting that His power was greater than their situation.

They had seen Him cast out demons. They knew He had powers that were not of natural origin. But they had never seen—or even heard of—anything like this. It's one thing to heal human sickness or even to order demons around. But to order the waves and the wind? To command the sea and the storm? That's a miracle of an entirely different order.

THE MIRACLE-MAN

¹They traveled across the sea to the land of Gerasa* *in Galilee, where the people were outsiders who had not seen Jesus before.* ²⁻³When Jesus came ashore there, He was immediately met by a man who was tortured by an evil spirit. This man lived in the cemeteries, and no one could control him—not even those who tried to tie him up or chain him. ⁴He had often been bound in chains, but his strength was so great that he could break the chains and tear the irons loose *from his feet and hands.* No one *and nothing* could subdue him. ⁵Day and night, he lurked among the tombs or *ran mad* in the hills, and *the darkness* made him scream or cut himself with *sharp-edged* stones. ⁶When this man saw Jesus coming in the distance, he ran to Him and fell to his knees in front of Him. ⁷⁻⁸Jesus started commanding the unclean spirit.

Jesus | Come out of that man, you wicked spirit!

Unclean Spirit | What's this all about, Jesus, Son of the Most High?
(shouting) | In the name of God, I beg You—don't torture me!

Jesus | ⁹What is your name?

Unclean Spirit | They call me "Legion," for there are thousands of us *in this body.*

5:1 The earliest manuscripts read "Gerasenes"; others read "Gadarenes."

¹⁰And then Legion begged Jesus again *to leave them alone,* not to send them out of the country.

¹¹*Since the Gerasenes were not Jews (who considered pigs to be unclean),* there happened to be a large herd of swine, *some 2,000 of them,* feeding on the hill nearby.

Unclean Spirit | ¹²Send us into those pigs *if You have to,* so that we
(begging) | may enter into them.

¹³Jesus granted the request. The darkness swept up out of the man and into the herd of pigs. And then they thundered down the hill into the water; and there they drowned, all 2,000 of them.

¹⁴The swineherds ran away, telling everybody they met what had happened. Eventually, a crowd of people came to see for themselves. ¹⁵When they reached Jesus, they found the man Legion had afflicted sitting quietly, sane and fully clothed; when they saw this, they were overwhelmed with fear *and wonder.*

¹⁶Those who had witnessed everything told the others what had happened: how Jesus had healed the man, how the pigs had rushed into the sea, and how they had destroyed themselves. ¹⁷*When they had heard the whole story,* the Gerasenes turned to Jesus and begged Him to go away.

¹⁸When Jesus climbed back into the boat, the cured demoniac asked if he could come and be with Him; but Jesus said no.

Jesus | ¹⁹Stay here; I want you to go back home to your own people and let them see what the Lord has done— how He has had mercy on you.

[20]So the man went away and began telling this news in the Ten Cities* region; and wherever he went, people were amazed by what he told them.

*T*wo things stand out in this story: how Jesus dealt with the demons and how the people responded to Jesus.

Although Jesus healed many people of demon possession during His ministry, this healing was unique. You see, this is the only time in the Gospels when Jesus seemed to listen to the pleading of a demon or a demon-possessed person. The demons immediately acknowledged Jesus as all-powerful; the possessed man's first reaction on seeing Jesus was to fall at His feet and call Him the "Son of the Most High." So it's unlikely that Jesus is negotiating with them in order to convince them to obey His orders. Although we can't assume to know why Jesus listened to their pleading, the effect was clear: the people in that region saw firsthand the power of evil and its ultimate destiny, namely, destruction.

The peoples' reaction to Jesus' decision to transfer the demons from the man into the herd of swine never could have been predicted. Instead of being pleased that they were now free from the terror of the demon-possessed man, the people in the town asked Jesus to leave. After all, the local economy took a pretty big hit when 2,000 of their choicest pigs rushed into the sea. But Kingdom priorities are always different from ours. Where God rules, people matter more than possessions.

5:20 Literally, the Decapolis

²¹After Jesus returned across the sea, a large crowd quickly found Him, so He stayed by the sea. ²²One of the leaders of the synagogue—a man named Jairus—came and fell at Jesus' feet, ²³begging Him to heal his daughter.

> **Jairus** | My daughter is dying, *and she's only 12 years old.* Please come to my house. Just place Your hands on her. I know that if You do, she will live.

²⁴Jesus began traveling with Jairus toward his home.

In the crowd pressing around Jesus, ²⁵there was a woman who had suffered continuous bleeding for 12 years, *bleeding that made her ritually unclean and an outcast according to the purity laws.* ²⁶She had suffered greatly; and although she spent all her money on her medical care, she had only gotten worse. ²⁷She had heard of this *Miracle-Man,* Jesus, so she snuck up behind Him in the crowd and reached out her hand to touch His cloak.

> **Woman** | ²⁸Even if all I touch are His clothes, I know I will be healed.
> *(to herself)*

²⁹*As soon as her fingers brushed His cloak,* the bleeding stopped. She could feel that she was whole again.

³⁰Lots of people were pressed against Jesus at that moment, but He immediately felt her touch; He felt healing power flow out of Him. *He stopped. Everyone stopped.* He looked around.

> **Jesus** | Who just touched My robe?

³¹His disciples broke the uneasy silence.

Disciples | Jesus, the crowd is so thick that everyone is touching You. Why do You ask, "Who touched Me?"

³²*But Jesus waited.* His gaze swept across the crowd to see who had done it. ³³At last, the woman—knowing He was talking about her—pushed forward and dropped to her knees. She was shaking with fear *and amazement.*

Woman | *I touched You.*

Then she told Him the reason why. ³⁴*Jesus listened to her story, and He nodded.*

Jesus | Daughter, you are well because you *dared to* believe. Go in peace, and stay well.

*J*esus occasionally instigated His own miracles. He would go up to someone, like a paralyzed man, and offer to heal him. More often, as in the case of Jairus's daughter, people would come to Jesus and ask for healings. But the woman in this story is unique because she received her healing without asking for it—simply by touching Jesus in faith. He was surrounded by crowds pressing in on every side, and crowds in first-century Palestine weren't particularly concerned about personal space. But Jesus knew that one person's touch was different, in a way that only He could perceive: one woman was touching Him deliberately, in hope and faith, knowing that He had the power to heal her.

³⁵While He was speaking, some members of Jairus's household pushed through the crowd.

Jairus's Servants *(to Jairus)*	Your daughter is dead. There's no need to drag the Teacher any farther.

³⁶Jesus overheard their words. Then He turned to look at Jairus.

Jesus | *It's all right.* Don't be afraid; just believe.

³⁷⁻³⁸Jesus asked everyone but Peter, James, and John (James's brother) to remain outside when they reached Jairus's home. Inside the synagogue leader's house, the mourning had already begun; and the weeping and wailing carried out into the street.
³⁹Jesus *and His three disciples* went inside.

Jesus | Why are you making all this sorrowful noise? The child isn't dead. She's just sleeping.

⁴⁰The mourners laughed *a horrible, bitter laugh and went back to their wailing.* Jesus cleared the house, so that only His three disciples, Jairus, and Jairus's wife were left inside with Him. They all went to where the child lay. ⁴¹Then He took the child's hand.

Jesus | Little girl, it's time to wake up.

⁴²Immediately, the 12-year-old girl opened her eyes, arose, and began to walk. Her parents could not believe their eyes.

| Jesus
(to the parents) | ⁴³Don't tell anybody what you've just seen. Why don't you give her something to eat? *I know she is hungry.* |

*J*esus at last arrived at the miracle He was asked to perform: the healing of Jairus's daughter. But He was too late—the girl was already dead. Although Jesus would later raise other dead people back to life, up to that point He had not yet performed such a powerful miracle. His ability to heal sickness was common knowledge, and the disciples had glimpsed His power over the natural world; but no one yet had an inkling of His power over the forces of life and death. He allowed only His closest disciples to see this first miracle of resurrection, and He urged everyone who did see it to keep it quiet. Nevertheless, it was this miracle that first demonstrated to those who saw it that He did indeed have power over death itself.

Mark 6

FLATBREAD AND FISH

¹Jesus went back into His own hometown where He had grown up, and His disciples followed Him there. ²When the Sabbath came, He went into the synagogue *in Nazareth* and began to teach *as He had done elsewhere*, and many of those who heard Him were astonished.

Those in the Synagogue | Where did He gain this wisdom? And what are all these stories we've been hearing about the signs and healings He's performed? *Where did He get that kind of power?* ³Isn't this *Jesus, the little boy we used to see in Joseph's carpenter shop*? Didn't He grow up to be a carpenter *just like His father?* Isn't He the son of Mary *over there* and the brother of James, Joses, Judas, Simon, and their sisters? *Who does He think He is?*

And when they had thought about it that way, they became indignant and closed themselves to His message.

Jesus *(seeing this)* | ⁴A prophet can find honor anywhere except in his hometown, among his own people, and in his own household.

⁵He could not do any of His great works among them except with a few of the sick, whom He healed by laying His hands upon them. ⁶He was amazed by the stubbornness of their unbelief.

Jesus went out among the villages teaching, [7]and He called the twelve to Him and began to send them out in pairs. He gave them authority over unclean spirits [8]and instructed them to take nothing with them but a staff: no money, no bread, no bag, [9]nothing but the sandals on their feet and the coat* on their back.

Jesus | [10]When you go into a house, stay there until it is time for you to leave that town. [11]And if someone will not accept you and your message, when you leave, shake off the dust of that place from your feet as a judgment against it. [On the day of judgment, that city will wish for the punishment of Sodom and Gomorrah.]*

[12]And so His disciples went out *into the countryside,* preaching the changed life* *as Jesus had taught them,* [13]casting out unclean spirits and anointing the sick with oil to heal them.

[14]Jesus had become so well known that King Herod received reports of all that Jesus was doing. Some were saying* that John the Prophet* had been raised from the dead and that these mighty works were the fruits of his resurrection. *Herod was stunned and shaken by this thought.*

Others
(disagreeing) | [15]No, this Jesus is Elijah, *returned to work on the earth.*

6:9 Literally, "not to wear two tunics."
6:11 Some of the earliest manuscripts omit this portion.
6:12 Literally, repentance
6:14 Some of the earliest manuscripts read "He was saying."
6:14 Literally, John who immersed to show repentance

And still others said He was another of the prophets.

> **Herod** | ¹⁶No, it is John, the prophet I beheaded, risen from
> *(to himself)* | the dead.

For the blood of John was on his hands. ¹⁷⁻¹⁸Herod had imprisoned John *in the days before Jesus began His teaching.* John had preached to Herod that he should not have married his own brother's wife, Herodias, for *so it is written in the Hebrew Scriptures:* It is not lawful for one to marry his brother's wife.*

¹⁹Herodias held a grudge against John and would have had him killed, but she couldn't. ²⁰Herod feared John as a holy and righteous man and did what he could to protect him. John taught hard truths,* and yet Herod found he usually liked hearing them.

So Herod had put John in prison instead of executing him; ²¹⁻²²*and there John sat until* Herod's birthday, when the governor held a great state dinner. That night, Herod's stepdaughter danced beautifully for the state officials; and the king proclaimed a solemn vow in the presence of *his honored guests,* military officers and some of the leading men of Galilee.

> **Herod** | Ask me whatever you wish, and I will grant it.
> ²³Whatever you want, I will give you—up to half my province.

²⁴She went out and consulted with her mother, *Herodias, who had only one great desire* and told her daughter what she must say.

6:17-18 Leviticus 18:16; 20:21
6:20 Some early manuscripts read "he did many things."

| Herod's Stepdaughter (*immediately, in response to Herod*) | ²⁵*There is only one thing I desire.* I want the head of John the Prophet*—right now—delivered to me on a platter. |

²⁶Herod was horrified, but he had sworn an oath and could not break his word in front of his invited guests. ²⁷So, immediately, he sent an executioner to the prison to behead John and bring them the head. ²⁸It was brought to the girl upon a platter, and she took it to her mother.

²⁹When John's disciples were told of this, they came for his body and gave it a proper burial.

³⁰Now the twelve returned from their travels and told Him what they had done, *who they had seen,* and how they had spread the news of God's kingdom.

| Jesus (*to the disciples*) | ³¹Let us go out into the wilderness for a while and rest ourselves. |

The crowds gathered as always, and Jesus and the twelve couldn't eat because so many people came and went. ³²They could get no peace until they boarded a boat and sailed toward a deserted place.

³³*But the people would not be put off so easily.* Those *along the shore* who recognized Jesus followed *along the coast.* People pushed out of all the cities and gathered ahead of Him ³⁴so that when Jesus came ashore and saw this crowd of people waiting for Him *in a place that should have been relatively deserted,* He was moved with compassion. They were like sheep without a shepherd.

6:25 Literally, John who immersed to show repentance.

He began to teach them many things ³⁵as the day passed; and at last, the disciples came to Jesus.

> **Disciples** | It is getting late, and there is nothing around for miles. ³⁶Send these people to the surrounding villages so they can buy something to eat.

> **Jesus** | ³⁷Why don't you give them something to eat?

> **Disciples**
> *(looking at Him)* | What? It would cost a fortune* to buy bread for these people!

> **Jesus** | ³⁸Does anyone have any bread? Go and see.

> **Disciples**
> *(returning from the crowd)* | There are five *pieces of flatbread* and two fish, *if that makes any difference.*

> **Jesus** | ³⁹⁻⁴⁰*Listen,* tell them to gather in smaller groups and sit on that green patch of grass.

And so the disciples gathered the people in groups of 100 or of 50, and they sat down.

⁴¹Jesus took the five pieces *of flatbread* and the two fish, looked up to heaven, thanked God for the food, and broke it. He gave the pieces to the disciples to distribute, ⁴²and all of the people ate until no one was hungry. ⁴³Then they gathered twelve baskets full of leftovers.

⁴⁴*That day,* 5,000 men ate their fill of the bread *when Jesus fed the hungry crowd.*

6:37 Literally, 200 denarii, Roman coins

*T*he disciples must have felt like they spent a lot of their time trying to bring Jesus back to earth. In the middle of His heavenly teachings, they were frequently reminding Him of ordinary concerns. In this case, their worries were especially mundane: they were out in a deserted place with thousands of people, and nobody had eaten anything all day. The disciples probably spent a long time discussing the problem among themselves before they finally decided to bother Jesus. Feeling irritable from hunger, with their stomachs growling loudly, they finally pulled Jesus aside to point out the obvious: everyone needed to go and eat something.

But Jesus, as usual, wasn't about to be distracted by the obvious. His answer must have irritated them even further: "Why don't you give them something to eat?" The disciples must have been dumbfounded. But Jesus was seeing a much bigger reality. He was deliberately creating a turning point in His ministry: He wanted to make them a part of His miracles. From recorders and observers, they would become participants. And so the disciples, not Jesus, told the people to sit down, passed out the food, and collected the leftovers after everyone had eaten until they were stuffed. The disciples must have felt pretty sheepish as they experienced how Jesus was making them a part of the miracle—despite their mundane concerns and their frustration with Him.

45Not long after, He sent His disciples out onto their boat to sail to Bethsaida on the other shore, and He sent the crowd away. 46After everyone had gone, He slipped away to pray on a mountain *overlooking the sea.*

⁴⁷When evening came, the boat was out on the sea; and He was alone on the land. ⁴⁸He saw that the disciples were making little progress because they were rowing against a stiff wind. Before daylight, He came near them, walking on the water, and would have passed by them. ⁴⁹Some of them saw Him walking on the surface of the water, thought He was a ghost, and cried out. ⁵⁰When they all saw Him, they were terrified.

| **Jesus** *(immediately calling out)* | Don't be frightened. Do you see? It is I. |

⁵¹*He walked across the water to the boat;* and as soon as He stepped aboard, the contrary wind ceased its blowing. They were greatly astonished; ⁵²for although they had just witnessed the miracle of Jesus feeding 5,000 with bread *and fish, and other signs besides*, they didn't understand *what it all meant* and their hearts remained hard.

*H*ow could the disciples still be in doubt about Jesus after having been part of so many miracles? Like the Israelites in the Old Testament, the disciples were discovering the truth that miracles don't produce faith. As Jesus so often pointed out in His healings, the process works the other way around: it's faith that produces miracles. Miracles are only signs—evidence of truth that you have to know before you can understand the miracle. As long as the disciples were still in doubt about who Jesus was, they would find their faith constantly challenged and frequently wavering, no matter how many miracles they witnessed or even participated in. It wouldn't be until after the resurrection, the greatest miracle of all, that they would come to recognize and believe in Jesus for who He was; and then, their hearts would at last become open.

⁵³When they finished their journey, they landed the boat in Gennesaret. ⁵⁴People at once recognized Jesus *as the Healer.* ⁵⁵Immediately, they hurried to collect the sick and infirm, bringing them to Him in beds if they had to, ⁵⁶laying them out in the markets of any village, city, or field where He might pass.

Gennesarites | Just let us touch the fringe of Your robe.

Even people who touch only it are made whole again.

NOT FOOD, BUT HEARTS

¹Then the Pharisees returned to talk with Jesus, and with them came some of the scribes *and scholars* from Jerusalem.

| Scribes and Scholars (seeing the disciples eating) | ²Your disciples are eating bread with defiled, unwashed hands. |

³Now *you need to know that* the Pharisees, and all Jews *for that matter,* held the tradition of their ancestors that hands must be washed before eating to avoid being ritually unclean. ⁴Likewise, they washed when they returned from the market and followed similar purity teachings as well, from the washing of their food to the washing of their bowls, cups, and kettles.

| Scribes and Pharisees | ⁵Why don't Your disciples follow the traditions passed down to us? Why do they eat their bread with defiled hands? |

| Jesus | ⁶Isaiah prophesied wisely about your religious pretensions when he wrote, |

> These people honor Me *with words* off their lips;
> meanwhile, their hearts are far from Me.
> ⁷Their worship is empty, *void of true devotion.*

> They teach a human commandment,
> *memorized and practiced by rote.**

⁸When you cling blindly to your own traditions [such as washing utensils and cups],* you completely miss God's command. ⁹Then indeed, you have perfected setting aside God's commands for the sake of your tradition. ¹⁰Moses gave you God's commandment: "Honor your father and your mother."* And also, "If you curse your father or your mother, you will be put to death."* ¹¹But *I hear one of* you say to your *aged* parents, "I've decided that the support you were expecting from me will now be the holy offering set aside for God." ¹²After that, he is not allowed to do anything for his parents. ¹³Do you think God wants you to honor your traditions that you have passed down *or His commandment of mercy, passed down directly from Him?* This is only one of many places where you are blind.

(to the crowd that had gathered) ¹⁴Listen, all of you, to this teaching. I want you to understand. ¹⁵There is nothing outside someone that can corrupt them. Only the things that come out of a person can corrupt them. [¹⁶All who have ears to hear, let them listen.]*

7:6-7 Isaiah 29:13
7:8 Some of the earliest manuscripts omit this portion.
7:10 Exodus 20:12; Deuteronomy 5:16
7:10 Exodus 21:17; Leviticus 20:9
7:16 Some manuscripts omit verse 16.

¹⁷When they had come in from the road, His disciples asked Him what He meant by this teaching.

Jesus | ¹⁸Do you mean you don't understand this one either? Whatever goes into people from outside can't defile them ¹⁹because it doesn't go into their hearts. Outside things go through their guts and back out, thus making all foods pure.* ²⁰No, it's what comes from within that corrupts. ²¹⁻²²It's what grows out of the hearts of people that leads to corruption: evil thoughts, immoral sex, theft, murder, adultery, greed, wicked acts, treachery, sensuality, jealousy, slander, pride, and foolishness. ²³All of these come from within, and these are the sins that truly corrupt a person.

*A*lthough Mark specifically states that Jesus was overriding the Old Testament dietary laws and declaring all foods pure, it would be a long time before the disciples were willing to act on that message. One of the biggest controversies in the early church was the question of dietary restrictions and how the Old Testament laws ought to be observed by Jewish and non-Jewish Christian believers. However, Jesus made it clear in this passage that His main concern had nothing to do with what people ate. Instead, He was concerned about the hearts of His followers.

7:19 The earliest texts say "Jesus declared all foods pure."

²⁴From there, Jesus and His followers traveled to the region of Tyre [and Sidon],* *on the Mediterranean coast.* He hoped to slip unnoticed into a house, but people discovered His presence. ²⁵*Shortly after He arrived,* a woman whose daughter was filled with an unclean spirit heard that He was there, so she came directly to Him and prostrated herself at His feet.

²⁶The woman was *not a Jew, but* a Syrophoenician (a Greek) by birth. *All the same,* she came to Jesus and begged Him to cast the unclean spirit out of her daughter.

Jesus *(shaking His head)*	²⁷I must feed the children first. It would do no good to take the children's bread and throw it to the dogs.
Syrophoenician Woman	²⁸Yes, Lord, but even the dogs under the table may eat of the children's crumbs.
Jesus *(smiling and nodding)*	²⁹This is a wise saying. Go back home. Your daughter is free of the spirit that troubled her.

³⁰And when she returned to her house, *she discovered that it was as Jesus had told her.* Her daughter lay on her bed, in her right mind, *whole and healthy.*

> *A*lthough Jesus at first answers the Greek woman harshly, He ultimately responded to her request. By healing her daughter,

---

7:24 Some manuscripts omit the bracketed words.

He demonstrated that God's loving presence has come to all people and not just to Jews. It's one of the first glimpses in this Gospel of the truth that would become clearer later—the truth that, through Jesus, God is making all people, and not just one chosen nation, clean and whole.

³¹Jesus traveled on His way through Tyre and Sidon, eventually returning to the region of the Sea of Galilee. From there, He pressed on to the area of the Ten Cities.* ³²*Among the sick* who were brought to Him was a man who was deaf and could barely speak at all, and those who brought him begged Jesus to lay His hands on the man. ³³Jesus took him aside from the crowd, alone, touched his ears with His fingers, and, after spitting on His fingers, Jesus touched the man's tongue. ³⁴Looking heavenward to God, Jesus sighed and commanded,

Jesus | Open up *and let this man speak.**

³⁵[Immediately,]* the man could hear, his tongue was loosed, and he spoke plainly. ³⁶Jesus ordered those *who had witnessed this* to tell no one; but the more He insisted, the more zealously people spread the word.

People | ³⁷He does everything so well! He even returns
(astonished) | sound to the deaf and mute.

7:31 Literally, the Decapolis
7:34 Aramaic *Ephphatha.*
7:35 Some of the earliest manuscripts omit this word.

*O*n His journey back from Tyre and Sidon, Jesus returned to an area where earlier He had performed an impressive miracle: the healing of the demon-possessed man.* Although the people of that town were eager to get rid of Him the first time, the testimony of the formerly possessed man had some effect because now the people of the Ten Cities were eager to bring a sick man to Jesus for healing.

Most of Jesus' healings took place with a simple word: He would speak, and the sick person would be well. But for this healing, He went through a series of actions. Why did Jesus, who could so easily heal without even seeing or touching a person, suddenly touch the man's ears and tongue and look up dramatically toward heaven before the man could be cured? Jesus wanted the man to have the chance to experience faith—the faith that Jesus often said was so important for all His healings. Since the man was deaf, Jesus communicated with him through signs so that the man could know what Jesus was doing. By touching the man's ears and tongue, Jesus demonstrated His intention to heal the parts that were broken. By looking up toward God, Jesus showed the man where His power came from. Only then, once the man had plenty of opportunity to anticipate the healing, did Jesus open his ears and free his tongue.

***Note** Mark 5:1-20

Mark 8

WHO AM I?

¹Once again, a huge crowd had followed them; and they had nothing to eat. So Jesus called His disciples together.

> **Jesus** | ²These people have been with Me for three days without food. They're hungry, and I am concerned for them. ³If I try to send them home now, they'll faint along the way because many of them have come a long, long way *to hear and see Me.*

> **Disciples** | ⁴Where can we find enough bread for these people in this desolate place?

> **Jesus** | ⁵How much bread do we have left?

> **Disciples** | Seven rounds of flatbread.

⁶*So, as before,* He commanded the people to sit down; and He took the rounds of flatbread and gave thanks for them and broke them. His disciples took what He gave them and fed the people. ⁷They also had a few small fish, which, after He had spoken a blessing, He likewise gave His followers to pass to the people. ⁸When all had eaten their fill and they had gathered up the food that remained, seven baskets were full.

⁹*On this occasion,* there were about 4,000 people who had eaten the food *that Jesus provided.* Jesus sent the crowd home;

¹⁰then, immediately, He got into a boat with His disciples and sailed away. Upon their arrival in Dalmanutha *in the district of Magdala,* ¹¹they were met by Pharisees—ready with their questions and tests—seeking some sign from heaven *that His teaching was from God.*

Jesus
(sighing with disappointment) | ¹²Why does this generation ask for a sign *that will cause them all to believe?* Believe Me when I say that you will not see one.

¹³He left the Pharisees and sailed across to the other shore.

¹⁴The disciples had forgotten to buy provisions, so they had only one round of flatbread among them. ¹⁵Jesus took this moment to warn them.

Jesus | Beware of the yeast of the Pharisees and the leaven of Herod.

The disciples *didn't understand what Jesus was talking about and* discussed it among themselves.

Some Disciples | ¹⁶What?

Other Disciples | He's saying this because we have run out of bread.

Jesus
(overhearing them) | ¹⁷⁻¹⁹Why are you focusing on bread? Don't you see yet? Don't you understand? You have eyes—why don't you see? You have ears—why don't you hear? Are you so hard-hearted?

Don't you remember when I broke the five rounds of flatbread among the 5,000? *Tell Me*, how many baskets of scraps were left over?

Disciples | Twelve.

Jesus | 20And how many were left when I fed the 4,000 with seven rounds?

Disciples | Seven.

Jesus | 21And still you don't understand?

22When they came into Bethsaida, a group brought a blind man to Jesus, and they begged Him to touch the man *and heal him.* 23So Jesus guided the man out of the village, *away from the crowd;* and He spat on the man's eyes and touched them.

Jesus | What do you see?

Blind Man
(opening his eyes) | 24I see people; but they look like trees, walking trees.

25Jesus touched his eyes again; and when the man looked up, he could see everything clearly.

26Jesus sent him away to his house.

Jesus
(to the healed man) | Don't go into town yet. [And don't tell anybody in town what happened here.]*

8:26 Some manuscripts omit this portion.

*B*ethsaida was the hometown of at least three of Jesus'
emissaries—Peter, Andrew, and Philip—and possibly James and
John as well. Jesus performed many miracles there, most notably
the feeding of the 5,000. However, this miracle—the healing of the
blind man—is the only miracle recorded in all the Gospels that was
done in stages instead of instantly.

Of course, there's no way to know for sure why Jesus chose to
heal this man partly before He healed Him entirely. Jesus frequently
linked faith, or lack of faith, with the healings. Bethsaida, too, was a
town He criticized for its lack of faith.*

Since Jesus had just rebuked His disciples for not understanding
the meaning of His miracles, it's likely He wanted to demonstrate to
them that their inability to see His purpose could be healed, too,
even if it took time.

²⁷As He traveled with His disciples into the villages of Caesarea
Philippi, He posed an *important* question to them.

Jesus | Who are the people saying I am?

²⁸They told Him *about the great speculation in the land concerning His
identity.*

Disciples | Some of them say *You are* John the Prophet,* others
say Elijah, while others say one of the prophets *of old.*

---

*Note Matthew 11:21-22
8:28 Literally, John who immersed to show repentance

Jesus *(pressing the question)*	²⁹And who do you say that I am?

Peter	You are the Liberating King, *God's Anointed One.*

Jesus	³⁰Don't tell anyone. *It is not yet time.*

³¹And He went on to teach them many things *about Himself:* how the Son of Man would suffer, how He would be rejected by the elders, chief priests, and scribes, how He would be killed, and how, after three days, *God would* raise Him from the dead.

³²He said all these things in front of them all, but Peter took Jesus aside.

Peter *(rebuking Him)*	*Lord, don't say this. This can't be true.*

*P*eter represents the best and worst in humanity. One day, Peter drops everything to become a follower of Jesus; the next, he's busy putting his foot in his mouth. Peter is always responding to his Liberator, frequently making mistakes, but never drifting far from Jesus' side. In this passage, Peter verbalizes God's word and Satan's temptation—almost in the same breath. Peter thought he understood who Jesus was, but he still had a lot to learn about what Jesus came to do.

Jesus *(seeing His disciples surrounding them)*	³³Get behind Me, you tempter! You're thinking only of human things, not of the things God has planned.

³⁴He gathered the crowd and His disciples alike.

Jesus | If any one of you wants to follow Me, you will have to give yourself up to God's plan, take up your cross, and do as I do. ³⁵For any one of you who wants to be rescued will lose your life, but any one of you who loses your life for My sake and for the sake of this good news will be liberated. ³⁶Really, what profit is there for you to gain the whole world and lose yourself *in the process*? ³⁷What can you give in exchange for your life? ³⁸If you are ashamed of Me and of what I came to teach to this adulterous and sinful generation, then the Son of Man will be ashamed of you when He comes in the glory of His Father along with the holy messengers *at the final judgment.*

Mark 9

Jesus
(continuing)

¹Truly, some of you who are here now will not experience death before you see the kingdom of God coming in *glory and* power.

²Six days after this saying, Jesus took Peter, James, and John and led them up onto a high mountaintop by themselves. There He was transformed ³so that His clothing became intensely white, brighter than any earthly cleaner could bleach them. ⁴Elijah and Moses appeared to them and talked with Jesus.

Peter
(to Jesus)

⁵Teacher, it's a great thing that we're here. We should build three shelters here: one for You, one for Moses, and one for Elijah.

⁶He *was babbling and* did not know what he was saying because they were terrified *by what they were witnessing*.
⁷Then a cloud surrounded them, and they heard a voice within that cloud.

Voice | This is My beloved Son. Listen to Him.

⁸All of a sudden, they looked about and all they had seen was gone. They stood alone on the mountain with Jesus.
⁹On their way back down, He urged them not to tell anyone what

they had witnessed until the Son of Man had risen from the dead, [10]so they kept it all to themselves.

*I*n what was probably one of the most spectacular events of their lives, Jesus' three closest disciples—Peter, James, and John—were given a glimpse of His divine nature. Mark doesn't usually record events with much attention to chronology; but in this case, he is careful to tell us that the transfiguration took place six days after Peter's confession of Jesus' identity. In a dramatic confirmation of the truth Peter had spoken then, the three disciples saw that Jesus is indeed the Anointed One of God. The veil of Jesus' human nature was pulled away, and the glory of His divinity shone through.

Alongside Jesus, the disciples saw two people whom they had never met, but instantly recognized: Moses and Elijah. Moses, who liberated the Hebrew slaves and received God's covenant atop Mount Sinai, represented God's law. Elijah represented all the prophets throughout history, since he was one of the greatest of them. The appearance of these two famous figures from the past showed that Jesus was the fulfillment of the law and the answer to all the promises of the prophets.

Finally, the disciples heard a voice from heaven—God's own voice—commanding them to listen to Jesus as His beloved Son. What an incredible confirmation of the truth that Peter had spoken in faith only six days before!

Disciples *(to one another)*	What does He mean, "Until the Son of Man is risen"?

(to Jesus) ¹¹Master, why do the scribes say that Elijah must come first?

Jesus *(thinking of John the Prophet)*	¹²Elijah does come first to restore all things. *They have it right.* But there is something else written in the Scriptures about the Son of Man: He will have to suffer and be rejected. ¹³*Here's the truth:* Elijah has come; and *his enemies treated him with contempt* and did what they wanted to him, just like it was written.

¹⁴When they reached the rest of the disciples, Jesus saw that a large crowd had gathered and that among them the scribes were asking questions. ¹⁵Right when the crowd saw Jesus, they were overcome with awe and surged forward immediately, *nearly running over the disciples.*

Jesus *(to the scribes)*	¹⁶What are you debating with My disciples? *What would you like to know?*

Father *(in the crowd)*	¹⁷Teacher, I have brought my son to You. He is filled with an unclean spirit. He cannot speak, ¹⁸and when the spirit takes control of him, he is thrown to the ground *to wail and moan,* to foam at the mouth, to grind his teeth, and to stiffen up. I brought him to Your followers, but they could do nothing with him. *Can You help us?*

Jesus	¹⁹Oh, faithless generation, how long must I be among you? How long do I have to put up with you? Bring the boy to Me.

²⁰They brought the boy toward Jesus; but as soon as He drew near, the spirit took control of the boy and threw him on the ground, where he rolled, foaming at the mouth.

Jesus *(to the father)*	²¹How long has he been like this?

Father	Since he was a baby. ²²This spirit has thrown him often into the fire and sometimes into the water, trying to destroy him. *I have run out of options; I have tried everything.* But if there's anything You can do, please, have pity on us and help us.

Jesus	²³"If there's anything You can do"? All things are possible, if you only believe.

Father *(crying in desperation)*	²⁴I believe, Lord. Help me to believe!

²⁵Jesus noticed that a crowd had gathered around them now. He issued a command to the unclean spirit.

Jesus	Listen up, you no-talking, no-hearing demon. I Myself am ordering you to come out of him now. Come out, and don't ever come back!

²⁶The spirit shrieked and caused the boy to thrash about; then it came out of the boy and left him lying as still as death. Many of those in the crowd whispered that he was dead. ²⁷But Jesus took the boy by the hand and lifted him to his feet.

²⁸Later, He and His disciples gathered privately in a house.

Disciples | Why couldn't we cast out that unclean spirit?
(to Jesus) |

Jesus | ²⁹That sort *of powerful spirit* can only be conquered with much prayer [and fasting].*

*T*he father of the possessed boy had some faith to begin with—enough to bring his son to Jesus and enough to ask for Jesus to heal him. But his faith was incomplete: this man asked hesitantly whether there was anything Jesus could do. In his desperation, the father recognized the limits of his faith. He believed—but was his faith strong enough for a healing? He wasn't sure, and that's why he begged for help. Perhaps that very desperation was enough faith; at any rate, Jesus immediately healed his son.

But later, the disciples showed the limitations of their faith when they drew Jesus aside for a private conversation. Having successfully healed many demon-possessed people when Jesus sent them out earlier, they were at a loss to know why they were completely unable to heal this little boy. Jesus' reply is cryptic and surprising: "That sort *of powerful spirit* can only be conquered with much prayer [and fasting]." It seems that although the disciples had faith that they could heal the boy, they were spiritually unprepared for the depth of evil that resides in the world. They needed to be saturated in the presence of God to face the challenge.

9:29 The earliest manuscripts omit this portion.

³⁰When they left that place, they passed secretly through Galilee.

Jesus   ³¹The Son of Man will be delivered into the hands
(to the disciples as   of the people, and they will kill Him. And after He
they traveled)   is killed, He will rise on the third day.

³²But again they did not understand His meaning, and they were
afraid to ask Him *for an explanation.*
    ³³At last, they came to Capernaum where they gathered in a
house.

Jesus | What was it I heard you arguing about along
          the way?

³⁴They *looked down at the floor and* wouldn't answer, for they had
been arguing among themselves about who was the greatest *of
Jesus' disciples.*

*I*t was only natural for them to wonder which of them would
be His right-hand man. And although it's hard to believe that the
three disciples who had just seen Jesus' glory revealed in the transfiguration would be part of such a petty discussion, how could they
have resisted it? After all, who had a better claim than they did to
being the greatest of Jesus' disciples?
    Fortunately, Jesus overheard what they were talking about and
He was quick to respond in mercy to correct their mistake.
Greatness in His eyes doesn't consist of seeing wonders or performing

> miracles or even fasting and praying. Instead, greatness is about humility and service. This is why He came. These are the heart of the kingdom of heaven.

³⁵He sat down with the twelve to teach them.

Jesus | Whoever wants to be first must be last, and *whoever wants to be the greatest* must be the servant of all.

³⁶He then called forward a child, set the child in the middle of them, and took the child in His arms.

Jesus | ³⁷Whoever welcomes a child like this in My name welcomes Me; and whoever welcomes Me is welcoming not Me, but the One who sent Me.

John
(to Jesus) | ³⁸Master, we saw another man casting out unclean spirits in Your name, but he was not one of our group. So we told him to stop what he was doing.

Jesus | ³⁹You shouldn't have said that. Anyone using My name to do a miracle cannot turn quickly to speak evil of Me. ⁴⁰Anyone who isn't against us is for us. ⁴¹The truth of the matter is this: anyone who gives you a cup of *cool* water to drink because you carry the name of your Liberator will be rewarded.
⁴²But if anyone turns even the smallest of My followers away from Me, it would be better for him

if someone had hung a millstone around his neck and flung him into the deepest part of the sea. ⁴³If your hand turns you away from the things of God, then you should cut it off. It's better to come into *eternal* life maimed than to have two hands and be flung into hell—[⁴⁴where the worm will not die and the fire will not be smothered.]*

⁴⁵If your foot trips you on the path, you should cut it off. It's better to come into *eternal* life crawling, than to have two feet and be flung into hell—[⁴⁶where the worm will not die and the fire will not be smothered.]*

⁴⁷And if your eye keeps you from seeing clearly, then you should pull it out. It's better to come into the kingdom of God with one eye than to have two eyes and be flung into hell, ⁴⁸where the worm will not die and the fire will not be smothered.* ⁴⁹Everyone will be salted with fire[, and every sacrifice will be seasoned with salt].* ⁵⁰Salt is a good thing; but if it has lost its zest, how can it be seasoned again? You should have salt within yourselves and peace with one another.

9:44 The earliest manuscripts omit verse 44, a quote from Isaiah 66:24.
9:46 The earliest manuscripts omit verse 46, a quote from Isaiah 66:24.
9:48 Isaiah 66:24
9:49 Some of the earliest manuscripts omit this portion.

No Longer Two People

¹From there, Jesus traveled to Judea and beyond the Jordan River; and He taught the crowds who gathered as was His custom.

²Some Pharisees came to Him to test Him *on His adherence to the law of Moses.*

Pharisees | Is it lawful for a husband to divorce his wife?

Jesus | ³What did Moses say to you?

Pharisees | ⁴Moses permitted us to write a certificate of dismissal and divorce her.*

Jesus | ⁵Moses gave you this law *as a concession* because of the hardness of your hearts. ⁶But truly, God created humans male and female in the beginning.* ⁷*As it is written in the Hebrew Scriptures,* "For this, a man will leave his father's and mother's *house* [to marry his wife],* ⁸and the two of them will become one flesh *and blood.*"* So they are no longer two people, but one. ⁹What God has joined together in this way, no one may sever.

10:4 Deuteronomy 24:1
10:6 Genesis 1:27; 5:2; the Hebrew name for the Book of Genesis is "In the beginning."
10:7 Some of the earliest manuscripts omit this portion.
10:8 Genesis 2:24

¹⁰In the privacy of their dwelling that evening, the disciples asked Him about this teaching; ¹¹and He went even further.

> **Jesus** | If any husband divorces his wife and then marries another woman, he commits adultery against her. ¹²And if a wife should divorce her husband and marry another, then she commits adultery *against him*.

*T*he Pharisees hoped to trip Jesus on a rather controversial question. His answer, however, is unusually straightforward. Instead of answering as they expect and taking a side in the popular debate, Jesus went back to the purpose and meaning of marriage—not just from a social perspective, but from a spiritual one.

¹³*When the crowd gathered again, parents and grandparents* had brought their children *and grandchildren* to see Jesus, hoping that He might *grant them His blessing* through His touch.

His disciples turned them all away; ¹⁴but when Jesus saw this, He was incensed.

> **Jesus**
> *(to the disciples)* | Let the children come to Me, and don't ever stand in their way, for this is what the kingdom of God is all about. ¹⁵Truly, anyone who doesn't accept the kingdom of God as a little child does can never enter it.

¹⁶Jesus gathered the children in His arms, and He laid His hands on them to bless them.

¹⁷When He had traveled on, a *young* man came and knelt *in the dust of the road* in front of Jesus.

Young Man | Good Teacher! What must I do to gain life in the world to come?

Jesus | ¹⁸You are calling Me good? *Don't you know that* God and God alone is good? ¹⁹*Anyway, why ask Me that question?* You know the Commandments *of Moses*: "Do not murder, do not commit adultery, do not steal, do not slander, do not defraud, and honor your father and mother."*

Young Man | ²⁰Yes, Teacher, I have done all these since I was a child.

²¹Then Jesus, looking at the young man, *saw that he was sincere* and responded out of His love for him.

Jesus | *Son,* there is still one thing you have not done. Go now. Sell everything you have and give the proceeds to the poor, so that you will have treasure in heaven. After that, come, follow Me.

²²The young man went away sick at heart at these words because he was very wealthy, ²³and Jesus looked around *to see if His disciples were understanding His teaching*.

10:19 Exodus 20:12-16; Deuteronomy 5:16-20

Jesus | Oh, it is hard for people with wealth to find their
(to His disciples) | way into God's kingdom!

Disciples | ²⁴*What?*
(amazed) |

Jesus | *You heard Me.* How hard it is to enter the kingdom of
God [for those who trust in their wealth]!*
²⁵I think you'll see camels squeezing through the
eye of a needle before you'll see the rich *celebrating
and dancing as they* enter into *the joy of* God's kingdom!

²⁶The disciples looked around at each other, whispering.

Disciples | Then who can be liberated?
(aloud to Jesus) |

Jesus | ²⁷For human beings it is impossible, but not for
(smiling and | God: God makes everything possible.
shaking His head) |

Peter | ²⁸Master, we have left behind everything we had to
follow You.

Jesus | ²⁹That is true. And those who have left their
houses, their lands, their parents, or their families
for My sake, and for the sake of this good news,
³⁰will receive all of this 100 times greater than they
have in this time—houses and farms and brothers,

10:24 Some manuscripts omit this portion.

sisters, mothers, and children, along with persecutions—and in the world to come, they will receive eternal life. ³¹But many of those who are first *in this world* shall be last *in the world to come,* and the last, first.

*T*his young man, like many wealthy people, was confident in his own abilities. He wanted to make sure that he would live well in the coming world, but he was not convinced that he was falling that short of the mark. And without humbly recognizing his own sinfulness and need in the face of God's goodness and perfection, it was indeed very hard for him to find the Kingdom.

This unnamed seeker was the only person in the Gospels outside of the twelve whom Jesus personally invited to follow Him. He was also the only person in the Gospels to walk away from that invitation.

Jesus now moved on. He was being drawn toward the holy city. Something wonderful and dangerous was ahead.

³²At length, they made their way toward Jerusalem. Jesus was walking ahead of them. As they neared the city, wonder and amazement filled them. But soon those who were following began to tremble.

Jesus
(taking the twelve aside)

³³Look, we are going up to Jerusalem; and there, the Son of Man is going to be delivered to the chief priests and the scribes. They shall seek His death and deliver Him to the outsiders *to carry out that*

sentence. ³⁴Then people will mock Him, spit upon Him, whip Him, and kill Him. But on the third day, He will rise again.

Two of the twelve—the sons of Zebedee *as they were known*—approached Jesus and pulled Him aside.

James and John	³⁵Teacher, will You do something for us if we ask it of You?
Jesus	³⁶What is it that you want?
James and John	³⁷*Master,* grant that we might sit on either side of You, one at Your right hand and one at Your left, when You come into the glory *of Your kingdom.*
Jesus	³⁸You don't know what it is you're asking. Can you drink from the cup I have to drink from or be washed* with the baptism that awaits Me?
James and John	³⁹We can.
Jesus	You will indeed drink from the cup I drink from and follow Me in what I must endure.* ⁴⁰But to sit at My right or at My left is an honor I cannot grant. That will be given to those for whom it has been prepared.

10:38 Literally, immersed
10:39 Literally, immersed with the immersion

⁴¹When the other ten heard about this request, they were angry with James and John; ⁴²but Jesus stopped them.

> **Jesus** | You know that among the nations of the world the great ones lord it over the little people and act like tyrants. ⁴³But that is not the way it will be among you. Whoever would be great among you must serve and minister. ⁴⁴Whoever wants to be great among you must be slave of all. ⁴⁵Even the Son of Man came not to be served but to be a servant—to offer His life as a ransom for others.

*H*is disciples were so convinced that He would rule as the conquering Liberator and King that they simply couldn't hear what He was saying about His trial and death. None of the disciples understood what He was telling them, and none of His predictions would become clear to them until after His resurrection.

In the meantime, several of His disciples were not only failing to understand His warnings about the things to come; they were missing His message on things right before their eyes. Jesus had already told them that to be great among His followers meant to become humble like a child; but James and John still thought that as two of His closest disciples, they could win worldly fame and power.

⁴⁶*By that time,* they had reached Jericho; and as they passed through the town, a crowd of people followed along. They came to a blind beggar, Bartimaeus, the son of Timaeus, who sat beside the *main*

road. ⁴⁷When he was told that Jesus of Nazareth was passing in that throng, he called out in a loud voice.

Bartimaeus | Jesus, Son of David, take pity on me and help me!

Disgusted by the blind man's public display, others in the crowd tried to silence him *until the Master passed.*

Some of the Crowd | ⁴⁸Be quiet. Shush.

Bartimaeus
(still louder) | Jesus, Son of David, have pity on me!

⁴⁹Jesus stopped where He stood. *The crowd stopped with Him.* He told those *near the front of the crowd* to call the blind man forward.

Some of the Crowd
(to Bartimaeus) | Good news! *Jesus has heard you. Listen*—He calls for you. Get up *and go to Him.*

⁵⁰Bartimaeus cast aside his *beggar's* robe and stepped forward, *feeling his way* toward Jesus.

Jesus | ⁵¹*Why did you call out to Me?* What do you want?

Bartimaeus | Teacher, I want to see.

Jesus | ⁵²Your faith has made you whole. Go in peace.

In that moment, Bartimaeus could see again; and from that time on, he followed Jesus.

*F*ew people in the Gospels showed as much persistence and eagerness in their desire to be healed as blind Bartimaeus. It took courage for him to ask Jesus to go out of His way for someone as seemingly unimportant as a blind beggar. Bartimaeus was not about to be swayed from his efforts to attract Jesus' attention. The discouragement from everyone around him only made him shout louder, determined to get the attention of the healer he'd heard about.

Jesus told the crowd to bring Bartimaeus to Him, and the blind man's actions demonstrated his faith. Beggars in first-century Palestine would spread a cloak on the ground in front of them to collect donations from compassionate passersby. It probably wasn't much; but for Bartimaeus, his cloak was everything he had. He threw it aside without a thought—probably along with the coins he had collected that day—because he was certain that once he'd met Jesus, he wouldn't need to be a beggar anymore.

THE IMPROMPTU PARADE

¹When they had gotten close to Jerusalem, near the two villages of Bethphage and Bethany and the Mount of Olives, Jesus sent two of His followers *ahead of them.*

> **Jesus** | ²Go to that village over there. As soon as you get into the town, you'll see a young colt tied that nobody has ever ridden. Untie it and bring it back *to Me.* ³If anybody *stops you and* asks what you're doing, just say, "The Lord needs it, and He will send it back right after He's done."

⁴*Everything happened just as Jesus had told them.* They found the colt in the street tied near a door, and they untied it.

> **Bystanders** | ⁵What are you doing?

⁶They answered as Jesus had instructed and were allowed to take it, ⁷so they brought the colt back to Jesus, piled garments on its back *to make a comfortable seat,* and Jesus rode the animal *toward Jerusalem.* ⁸*As they traveled,* people cast their cloaks onto the road and spread out leafy branches, which they had brought from the fields *along the way.* ⁹People walked ahead of them, and others followed behind.

> **People** | Hosanna! *Rescue us now, Lord!*
> (shouting)

*T*his impromptu parade fulfilled the Hebrew Scriptures. "Hosanna" means, "Rescue us, Lord." The people sang this and other words out of the Psalms to praise and honor Jesus.

People | Hosanna!
(singing) |
   Blessed be the One who comes in the name
      of the Eternal One!*
      ¹⁰And blessed is the kingdom of our father
         David, which draws closer *to us today*!
   Hosanna in the highest heavens!

*L*ess than a week before He would be crucified, Jesus entered Jerusalem for the last time and acted in ways His followers expected of the Liberating King. But as He accepted the praise of the crowds, He radically redefined their every expectation. His description to His disciples of where they would find the colt He would ride, and how they should get it, had an air of prophecy and supernatural knowledge. More overtly, He rode a donkey instead of being carried into town on the backs of servants (in a litter as a conquering king would have done), fulfilling the prophecy in Zechariah 9:9 that the King would come riding a donkey.* After all, donkeys were a poor man's mount; and Jesus wanted to identify with the poor. Even in this triumphal entry, Jesus made it clear that He did not intend to conquer and rule in a worldly way.

11:9 Psalm 118:26
***Note** Zechariah 9:9

However, the grandeur of His entrance was augmented by the response of the crowds who followed Him. For most of His ministry, Jesus avoided crowds and suppressed rumors and praise about the miracles He had done. Now, for the first time, He allowed the crowds to voice their excitement about who He was and all that He'd been doing.

¹¹*To the sound of this chanting,* Jesus rode through the gates of Jerusalem and up to the temple. He looked around, *taking note;* but because evening was coming, He and the twelve went back to Bethany *to spend the night.*

¹²The next morning, when they departed Bethany and *were traveling back to the city,* Jesus was hungry. ¹³Off in the distance, He saw a fig tree fully leafed out, so He headed toward it to see if it might have any ripe fruit. But when He reached it, He found only leaves because the fig season had not yet come.

¹⁴As the disciples listened, *Jesus pronounced a curse on the tree.*

Jesus | No one will ever eat fruit from your branches again.

*T*his is the only time in the Gospels when Jesus used His supernatural power to destroy rather than to heal; and on the surface, He seems to have done so mostly out of irritation.

The tree was "fully leafed out"—a stage that usually would come after figs were ripe and not before. So the tree was already barren: its leaves had grown profusely before their time, without the tree having produced fruit. Because the tree looked as though it ought to have fruit but didn't, it was a perfect illustration of people who believed they had the good fruit of righteousness even though their actions were void of true compassion and love, as empty and useless as leaves. And so Jesus cursed the fig tree, not out of anger with the tree itself, but as a warning to hypocrites who thought their appearance was more important than the fruit of their actions.

¹⁵They continued into Jerusalem *and made their way up to the temple.*

Upon reaching the temple *that morning,* Jesus dealt with those who were selling and buying *animals for sacrifices* and drove them out of the area. He turned over the tables of those who exchanged money *for the temple pilgrims* and the seats of those selling birds, ¹⁶and He *physically* prevented anyone from carrying anything through the temple.

Jesus *(to those who were listening)*	¹⁷Didn't the prophets write, "My house will be called a house of prayer, for all the people,"* but you have made it into a "haven for thieves"*?

*A*t the temple, Jesus was confronted with a scene that shocked Him. So He made a scene Himself. But He wasn't merely acting out; He had a message and, like the prophets of old, this

---

11:17 Isaiah 56:7
11:17 Jeremiah 7:11

message was better seen than heard. He acted decisively and with great emotion against those who had turned God's house into a place where pilgrims were exploited. You see, the temple leadership had allowed profiteers and merchants to set up shop in the court of the Gentiles, and they were making ridiculous profits. For the people who came long distances to worship, it was a normal practice to have merchants selling animals for them to sacrifice. What was not normal and what was immoral was where and how they transacted business. Jesus took issue with robbers profiteering in His Father's house.

¹⁸The chief priests and the scribes heard these words *and knew Jesus was referring to them,* so they plotted His destruction. They had grown afraid of Him because His teachings struck the crowds into astonishment.

¹⁹When evening came, Jesus [and His followers]* left the city again. ²⁰The next morning *on the way back to Jerusalem,* they passed a tree that had withered down to its very roots.

Peter *(remembering)*	²¹That's the fig tree, Teacher, the one You cursed *just yesterday morning.* It's withered away *to nothing*!

Jesus	²²Trust in God. ²³*If you do,* honestly, you can say to this mountain, "Mountain, uproot yourself and throw yourself into the sea." If you don't doubt, but trust that what you say will take place, then it will

---

11:19 Some of the earliest manuscripts read "he."

happen. [24]So listen to what I'm saying: Whatever you pray for or ask *from God*, believe that you'll receive it and you will. [25]When you pray, if you remember anyone who has wronged you, forgive him so that God above can also forgive you. [[26]If you don't forgive others, don't expect God's forgiveness.]*

[27]As they arrived in Jerusalem and were walking in the temple, the chief priests, scribes, and elders came to Jesus [28]and asked Him a question.

> **Leaders** | Tell us, who has given You the authority to say and do the things You're saying and doing?

> **Jesus** | [29]I will answer your question, if you will answer one for Me. Only then will I tell you who gives Me authority to do these things. [30]Tell Me, when John was ritually cleansing* *for the forgiveness of sins*, was his authority from heaven or was it merely human?

[31]The priests, scribes, and elders huddled together to think through an answer.

> **Leaders**
> *(to themselves)* | If we say, "It must have been from heaven," *then Jesus will jump on us.* He'll ask, "Then why didn't you listen to him and follow him?" [32]But if we say, "John's cleansing was only human," the people will

---

11:26 Some of the earliest manuscripts omit verse 26.
11:30 Literally, immersing, to show repentance

be up in arms because they think John was a prophet *sent by God*.

    (responding to Jesus) [33]We don't know what to tell You.

Jesus | *All right*, then don't expect Me to tell you where I get the authority to say and do these things.

*T*he question that the religious leaders asked Jesus—where His authority came from—is, in many ways, *the* central question about Jesus. They were probably referring to His overturning the tables in the temple and subsequently challenging a business practice that was perfectly acceptable to all the religious leaders. But there was more! What gave Him the right to heal people on the Sabbath or teach people about God? What gave Him the right to do all those miracles and cast out demons? Who exactly did He think He was—and where did His authority come from? Was He, as people were saying, the Liberating King? Did He plan to become king? They thought they could trap Him with this question: if He claimed His authority was from God, then they could argue that God would not endorse someone who broke His laws; but if He said His authority was His own, then it would be easy to get Him in trouble with the crowds that followed Him and perhaps even with the Roman governor.

    Jesus, however, had a better idea. He issued a challenge: I'll tell you what you want to know if you'll answer this one first. But He asked them an impossible question—impossible not because they didn't know the answer, but because they couldn't say the answer.

THE MOST IMPORTANT COMMANDMENT

¹Then He told a story.

Jesus | There was a man who established a vineyard. *He planted and staked the grapes;* he put up a wall around it to fence it in; he dug a pit for a winepress; he built a watchtower. *When he had finished this work,* he leased the vineyard to some tenant farmers and went away to a distant land.

²When the grapes were in season, he sent a slave to the vineyard to collect *his rent*—his share of the fruit. ³But the farmers grabbed the slave, beat him, and sent him back to his master empty-handed. ⁴The owner sent another slave, and this slave the farmers beat over the head and sent away dishonored. ⁵A third slave, the farmers killed. This went on for some time, with the farmers beating some of the messengers and killing others *until the owner had lost all patience.* ⁶He had a son whom he loved above all things, and he said to himself, *"When these thugs see my son, they'll know he carries my authority.* They'll have to respect him."

⁷*But when the tenant farmers saw the owner's son coming,* they said among themselves, "Look at this! It's the son, the heir to this vineyard. If we kill him,

then the land will be ours!" ⁸So they seized him and killed him and threw him out of the vineyard.

⁹Now, what do you suppose the owner will do *when he hears of this*? He'll come and destroy these farmers, and he'll give the land to others.

¹⁰Haven't you read the Scriptures? *As the psalmist says,*

> "The stone that the builders rejected
>   has become the very stone that holds
>   together the entire foundation.
> ¹¹This is the work of the Eternal One;
>   and it is marvelous in our eyes."*

¹²The priests, scribes, temple leaders, and elders knew the story was directed against them. They couldn't figure out how to lay their hands on Jesus then because they were afraid the people *would rise up against them.* So they left Him alone, and they went away *furious.*

*S*tunning. In their minds, judgment would come upon their enemies, and they would be justified. The implication that they themselves would face judgment, not to mention the imminent threat the ending of the story conveys, went against everything they believed about themselves and about God. And so, blinded by their own anger, they acted exactly as He said they would, despite the warning He gave them about what the ultimate consequence would be.

12:11 Psalm 118:22-23

¹³Then some Pharisees and some of Herod's supporters banded together to try to entrap Jesus. ¹⁴They came to Him and complimented Him.

> **Pharisees** | Teacher, we know You are truthful *in what You say* and that You don't play favorites. You're not worried about what anyone thinks of You, so You teach with total honesty what God would have us do. *So tell us*: is it lawful that we Jews should pay taxes to the Roman emperor or not? ¹⁵Should we give or not?

> **Jesus**
> *(seeing through their ruse)* | Why do you test Me like this? Listen, bring Me a coin* so that I can take a look at it.

¹⁶When they had brought it to Him, He asked them another question.

> **Jesus** | *Tell Me*, whose picture is on this coin? And of whom does this inscription speak?

> **Pharisees** | Caesar, of course.

> **Jesus** | ¹⁷Then give to the emperor what belongs to the emperor. And give God what belongs to God.

They could not think of anything to say to His response.

12:15 Literally, denarius, a Roman coin

*J*esus answered their question. But since He knew the spiritual state of their hearts, He turned the question back on them. It wasn't about taxes or loyalty to the emperor. It was about knowing and living faithfully to the one true God.

¹⁸Later, a group of Sadducees, *Jewish religious leaders* who didn't believe the dead would be resurrected, came to test Jesus.

Sadducees | ¹⁹Teacher, the law of Moses tells us, "If a man's brother dies, leaving a widow without sons, then the man should marry his sister-in-law and *try to* have children with her in his brother's name."*

²⁰Now here's the situation: there were seven brothers. The oldest took a wife and left her a widow with no children. ²¹So the next oldest married her, left her a widow, and again there were no children. So the next brother married her and died, and the next, *and the next*. ²²Finally all seven brothers had married her, but none of them had conceived children with her, and at last she died also.

²³Tell us then, in the resurrection [when humans rise from the dead]*, whose wife will she be? For all seven of them married her.

Jesus | ²⁴You can't see the truth because you don't know the Scriptures well and because you don't really

---

12:19 Deuteronomy 25:5
12:23 Some manuscripts omit this portion.

believe that God is powerful. [25]The answer is this: when the dead rise, they won't be married or given in marriage. They'll be like the messengers in heaven, *who are not united with one another in marriage.* [26]But how can you fail to see the truth of resurrection? Don't you remember in the Book of Moses how God talked to Moses out of a burning bush and what God said to him then? "I am the God of Abraham, the God of Isaac, and the God of Jacob."* *"I am," God said. Not "I was."* [27]So God is not the God of the dead, but of the living. You are sadly mistaken.

[28]One of the scribes *who studied and copied the Hebrew Scriptures* overheard this conversation and was impressed by the way Jesus had answered.

Scribe | Tell me, Teacher. What is the most important thing that God commands *in the law*?

Jesus | [29]The most important commandment is this: "Hear, O Israel, the Eternal One is our God, and the Eternal One is the only God. [30]You should love the Eternal, your God, with all your heart, with all your soul, with all your mind, and with all your strength."* [31]The second *great commandment* is this: "Love others in the same way you love yourself."* There are no commandments more important than these.

12:26 Exodus 3:6,15
12:30 Deuteronomy 6:4-5
12:31 Leviticus 19:18

Although Jesus was asked for only the single most impor-tant commandment, He answered by naming two commands: love God and love others. He included both because these two teachings can never be really separated from each other. Some people think they can love God and ignore the people around them, but Jesus frequently made it clear that loving God apart from His people is completely impossible.

Scribe | ³²Teacher, You have spoken the truth. For there is one God and only one God, ³³and to love God with all our heart and soul and mind and strength and to love our neighbors as ourselves are more impor-tant than any burnt offering or sacrifice *we could ever give.*

³⁴Jesus heard that the man had spoken with wisdom.

Jesus | *Well said; if you understand that,* then the kingdom of God is closer than you think.

Nobody asked Jesus any more questions after that.

³⁵Later, Jesus was teaching in the temple.

Jesus | Why do the scribes say that the Liberating King is the son of David? ³⁶*In the Psalms,* David himself was led by the Holy Spirit to sing,

"The Eternal One said to my Lord,
'Sit at My right hand,
in the place of power and honor,
And I will gather Your enemies together,
lead them in on hands and knees,
and You will rest Your feet on their
backs.' "*

³⁷If David calls the Liberator "Lord," how can He be his son?

The crowd listened to Him with delight.

Jesus | ³⁸Watch out for the scribes *who act so religious*—who like to be seen in pious clothes and to be spoken to respectfully in the marketplace, ³⁹who take the best seats in the synagogues and the place of honor at every dinner, ⁴⁰who spend widows' inheritances and pray long prayers to impress others. These are the kind of people who will be condemned above all others.

⁴¹Jesus sat down opposite the treasury, where people came to bring their offerings, and He watched as they came and went. Many rich people threw in large sums of money, ⁴²but a poor widow came and put in only two small coins* worth only a fraction of a cent.*

12:36 Psalm 110:1
12:42 Greek lepta, a coin worth an insignificant amount
12:42 Literally, kodrantes, a Roman penny

Jesus
*(calling His
disciples together)*

⁴³Truly, this widow has given a greater gift than any other contribution. ⁴⁴All the others gave a little out of their great abundance, but this poor woman has given God everything she has.

Mark 13

LEARN FROM THE FIG TREE

¹As Jesus left the temple *later that day,* one of the disciples noticed *the grandeur of Herod's temple.*

Disciple | Teacher, I can't believe the size of these stones! Look at these magnificent buildings!

Jesus | ²Look closely at these magnificent buildings. *Someday* there won't be one of these great stones left on another. Everything will be thrown down.

³They took a seat on the Mount of Olives, across *the valley* from the temple; and Peter, James, John, and Andrew asked Jesus to explain His statement to them privately.

Peter, James, John, and Andrew | ⁴Don't keep us in the dark. When will the temple be destroyed? What sign will let us know that it's about to happen?

Jesus | ⁵Take care that no one deceives you. ⁶Many will come claiming to be Mine, saying, "I am the One," and they will fool lots of people. ⁷You will hear of wars, or that war is coming, but don't lose heart. These things will have to happen, although it won't mean the end yet. ⁸Tribe will rise up against tribe,

nation against nation, and there will be earth-
quakes in place after place and famines. These are a
prelude to "labor pains" *that precede the temple's fall.*

⁹Be careful, because you will be delivered to trial
and beaten in the places of worship. Kings and gover-
nors will stand in judgment over you as you speak in
My name. ¹⁰The good news *of the coming kingdom of God*
must be delivered first in every land and every language. ¹¹When people bring you up on charges and it
is your time to defend yourself, don't worry about
what message you'll deliver. Whatever comes to your
mind, speak it, because the Holy Spirit will inspire it.

¹²*But it will get worse.* Brothers will betray each
other to death, and fathers will betray their children. Children will turn against their parents and
cause them to be executed. ¹³Everyone will hate you
because of your allegiance to Me. But if you're
faithful until the end, you will be rescued.

¹⁴On the day that you see the desecration of our
most holy place* [described by Daniel the prophet]*
where it is out of place,

Let the one who reads *and hears* understand,

Jesus | Whoever is in Judea should flee for the mountains.
¹⁵The person on the rooftops shouldn't reenter the
house to get anything, ¹⁶and the person working in
the field shouldn't turn back to grab his coat. ¹⁷It

13:14 Literally, "abomination of desolation," Daniel 9:27; 11:31; 12:11
13:14 The earliest manuscripts omit this portion.

will be horrible for women who are pregnant, or who are nursing their children when those days come. [18]And pray that you don't have to run for your lives in the winter. [19]When those days come, there will be suffering like nobody has seen from the beginning of the world that God created until now and it never will be like this again. [20]And if the Lord didn't shorten those days for the sake of the ones He has chosen, then nobody would survive them.

[21]If anyone tells you in those days, "Look, there is the Liberating King!" or "Hey, that must be Him!" don't believe them. [22]False liberators and prophets will pop up *like weeds,* and they will work signs and perform miracles that would entice even God's chosen people, if that were possible. [23]So be alert, and remember how I have warned you.

[24-25]*As Isaiah said,* in the days after that great suffering,

"The sun will refuse to shine,
      and the moon will hold back its light.
[25]The stars in heaven will fall,
      and the powers in the heavens will be
      shaken."*

[26]Then you will see *(as Daniel predicted)* "the Son of Man coming in the clouds,"* *clothed* in power

---

13:24-25 Isaiah 13:10; 34:4
13:26 Daniel 7:13

and majesty. [27]And He will send out His heavenly messengers, and gather together to Himself those He has chosen from the four corners of the world, from every direction and every land.

*E*ven though the disciples had never understood Jesus' warnings about His coming death, they couldn't help but notice that something was in the air during this week between His entry into Jerusalem and His crucifixion. Surely the moment they'd been waiting for—the moment when Jesus would reveal Himself as the Liberating King—couldn't be far off.

As the disciples were asking about the temple, they were also thinking of promises about the Liberator. But for Jesus, everything now was connected to His imminent death and resurrection. Even as He predicted the temple's fall—an event that did occur about 40 years later—and spoke of His second coming, He was still thinking about His death. After all, resurrection can't happen unless something dies first. And the old world, too, will have to die before the world is made new.

Jesus | [28]Learn this lesson from the fig tree: When its branch is new and tender and begins to put forth leaves, you know that summer must be near. [29]In the same way, when you see *and hear* the things I've described to you taking place, you'll know the time is drawing near. [30]It's true—this generation will not pass away before all these things have happened.

³¹Heaven and earth may pass away, but these words of Mine will never pass away.

³²*Take heed:* no one knows the day or hour when the end is coming. The messengers in heaven don't know, nor does the Son. Only the Father knows.

³³So be alert. Watch for it, [and pray,]* for you never know when that time might approach.

³⁴This situation is like a man who went on a journey; and when he departed, he left his servants in charge of the house. Each of them had his own job to do; and the man left the porter to stand at the door, watching. ³⁵So stay awake, because no one knows when the master of the house is coming back. It could be in the evening or at midnight or when the rooster crows or in the morning. ³⁶*Stay awake;* be alert, so that when he suddenly returns, the master won't find you sleeping.

³⁷The teaching I am giving *the four of* you now is for everyone *who will follow Me*: stay awake, *and keep your eyes open.*

*M*any Christians have tried to use this chapter to predict exactly when Jesus will come and how the world will end. But to do that is to do exactly the opposite of what Jesus intended when He spoke these words. He made it very clear that He doesn't want anyone to use this description of signs to predict an exact time and date

---

13:33 Some manuscripts omit this portion.

for His coming; even He Himself doesn't know that time and date, and no one else needs to know either. In fact, it's probably to our benefit not to know. Instead, the purpose was to warn them—and us—to stay ready and alert.

Mark 14

The Son of Man Goes to His Fate

For the Jews, no time of the year was more important than the Passover. Anyone who could make the journey came to Jerusalem during this celebration of the rescue of the Hebrew slaves from Egypt. As the city of Jerusalem filled with Jewish pilgrims and as the Roman soldiers stationed in Jerusalem stood ready to keep order, excitement and tension began to build.

¹The Passover and the Feast of Unleavened Bread were two days away. *The Jewish leaders*—the chief priests and the scribes—gathered to discuss how they might secretly arrest Jesus and kill Him. *But some were cautious.*

Jewish Leaders | ²We can't do it during the festivals. It might create an uproar. *There is too much potential for trouble.*

³While Jesus was eating dinner in Bethany at the house of Simon the leper, a woman came into the house carrying an alabaster flask filled with a precious, sweet-smelling ointment made from spikenard. She came to Jesus, broke the jar, and gently poured out the perfume onto His head.

⁴Some of those around the table were troubled by this and grumbled to each other.

Dinner Guests | Why did she waste this precious ointment? ⁵We
could have sold this ointment for almost a year's
wages,* and the money could have gone to the poor!

Their *private concerns* turned to public criticism against her.

Jesus | ⁶Leave her alone. Why are you attacking her? She
has done a good thing. ⁷The poor will always be
with you, and you can show kindness to them whenever you want. But I won't always be with you. ⁸She
has done what she could for Me—she has come to
anoint My body and prepare it for burial. ⁹Believe
Me when I tell you that this act of hers will be told
in her honor as long as there are people who tell
the good news.

*L*ike many people today, the disciples couldn't see any
value in something apart from its practical purpose; and pouring so
much perfume on Jesus was obviously a waste. We as Christians
need to be careful about what we call wasteful or useless because in
God's kingdom, small and apparently useless actions may have
great meaning. Clearly, this experience was a meaningful one for
Jesus. The woman was demonstrating her love for Him with an
abandon and an emotional commitment that few people had ever
shown, and He appreciated her love and her faith. To Him, it was
more than a gesture; it was a practical preparation for His imminent

---

14:5 Literally, more than 300 denarii

> death and burial. No one else there could see what use her action was; but to Jesus, it was incredibly precious—so much so that He promised to make sure her action was never forgotten.

¹⁰It was after this that Judas Iscariot, one of the twelve, went to meet the chief priests with the intention of betraying Jesus to them. ¹¹When they heard what he proposed, they were delighted and promised him money. So from that time on, Judas *thought and waited and* sought an opportunity to betray Jesus.

¹²On the first day of the Feast of Unleavened Bread, the customary day when the Passover lamb is sacrificed, His disciples wondered *where they would celebrate the feast.*

Disciples | Where do You want us to go and make preparations for You to eat the Passover meal?

¹³So *again* He sent two of His disciples ahead and told them to watch for a man carrying a jar of water.

Jesus | Follow that man; ¹⁴and wherever he goes in, say to the owner of the house, "The Teacher asks, 'Where is the guest room where I can eat the Passover meal with My disciples?'" ¹⁵He will take you upstairs and show you a large room furnished and ready. Make our preparations there.

¹⁶So the two left and went into the city. All was as Jesus had told them, and they prepared the meal in the upper room.

¹⁷That evening Jesus and the twelve arrived *and went into the upper room*; ¹⁸and each reclined around the table, *leaning upon an elbow* as he ate.

> **Jesus** | I tell you in absolute sincerity, one of you eating with Me tonight is going to betray Me.

¹⁹The twelve were upset. *They looked around at each other.*

> **Disciples** | Lord, it's not I, is it?
> *(one by one)* |

> **Jesus** | ²⁰It is one of you, the twelve—one of you who is dipping your bread in the same dish that I am.
> ²¹The Son of Man goes *to His fate*. That has already been predicted in the Scriptures. But still, it will be terrible for the one who betrays Him. It would have been better for him if he had never been born.

²²As they ate, Jesus took bread, offered a blessing, and broke it. He handed the pieces to His disciples.

> **Jesus** | Take this [and eat it].* This is My body.

²³He took a cup *of wine*; and when He had given thanks *for it*, He passed it to them, and they all drank from it.

14:22 Some manuscripts omit this portion.

Jesus | ²⁴This is My blood, a covenant* poured out on behalf of many. ²⁵Truly, I will never taste the fruit of the vine again until the day when I drink it new in the kingdom of God.

*T*he church has always regarded this moment of the Last Supper, a moment commemorated in services all over the world for thousands of years, as one of the most important moments in Jesus' life. Exactly what Jesus meant by calling the bread and wine His body and blood has been debated over the centuries; the full meaning of that statement remains a mystery. Still, Christians have always agreed that whenever this moment is remembered and celebrated, the Liberating King is present with His people. By eating the bread and drinking the wine, we as believers participate not only in this supper but also in His death and resurrection because the bread is torn and the wine is poured, just as His body was torn and His blood poured out.

Sometimes it's easier for us to understand these mysteries in a spiritual and allegorical sense. But to do that too much is to forget the incarnation. Just as Jesus' physical body housed the Spirit of God, the physicality of the bread and wine has a spiritual significance. Otherwise, we wouldn't need to eat the bread and drink the wine to celebrate this moment—it would be enough for us to read the story and remember what happened. But we, too, are physical as well as spiritual; and our physical actions can have spiritual importance.

14:24 Some manuscripts read "the new covenant."

²⁶*After the meal,* they sang a psalm and went out *of the city* to the Mount of Olives.

Jesus | ²⁷All of you will desert Me tonight. It was written *by Zechariah,*

> "I will strike the shepherd,
>   and the sheep will scatter."*

²⁸But when I am raised up, I will go ahead of you to Galilee.

Peter | ²⁹It doesn't matter who else turns his back on You. I
(protesting) | will never desert You.

Jesus | ³⁰Peter, mark My words. This very night before the cock crows twice, you will have denied Me three times.

Peter | ³¹*No, Teacher.* Even if it means that I have to die
(insisting) | with You, I'll never deny You.

All the other disciples said similar things.
　　³²They came *at length* to a garden called Gethsemane.

Jesus | Stay here. I'm going *a little farther* to pray *and to think.*

14:27 Zechariah 13:7

³³He took Peter, James, and John with Him; *and as they left the larger group behind,* He became distressed and filled with sorrow.

> **Jesus** | ³⁴My heart is so heavy; I feel as if I could die. Wait here for Me, and *stay awake to* keep watch.

³⁵He walked on a little farther. Then He threw Himself on the ground and prayed for deliverance from what was about to come.

> **Jesus** | ³⁶Abba, Father, I know that anything is possible for You. Please take this cup away so I don't have to drink from it. But whatever happens, let Your will be done—not Mine.

³⁷He got up, went back *to the three,* and found them sleeping.

> **Jesus**
> *(waking Peter)* | Simon, are you sleeping? Couldn't you wait with Me for just an hour? ³⁸Stay awake, and pray that you aren't led into a trial of your own. *It's true*—even when the spirit is willing, the body can betray it.

³⁹He went away again, *threw Himself on the ground,* and prayed again the same prayer as before—*pleading with God but surrendering to His will.*

⁴⁰He came back and found the three asleep; *and when He woke them,* they didn't know what to say to Him.

⁴¹After He had gone away and prayed for a third time, *He returned to find them slumbering.*

Jesus | Again? Still sleeping and getting a good rest? Well, that's enough sleep. The time has come; the Son of Man is betrayed into the hands of sinners. ⁴²Get up now, and let's go. The one who is going to betray Me is close by.

*I*n the moments before Jesus' death, Mark gives us an intimate glimpse into Jesus' humanity. For anyone who's ever wondered whether Jesus really knew what it felt like to be human and afraid, this story proves He did. Jesus knew exactly what was about to happen to Him and exactly how bad it would be. We all know to some extent what it is like to face pain and suffering. We can't help but be afraid and plead with God to take it away. So, too, Jesus had been anticipating this suffering for a long time. And now that the time for it had come, He felt all the natural human emotions.

Most amazing of all is the prayer Jesus said in that moment: "Please take this cup away *so I don't have to drink from it.*" Even though, in His divine nature, He knew what was going to happen— what must happen—He still asked, in His human nature, for a reprieve. At the same time, He submitted His human desires and will to the plan of His Father: in order to experience fully what it means to be human, He had to go through even this—denying Himself and what He wanted to face certain torture and death.

⁴³Before He had finished talking, Judas (one of the twelve) approached with a large group of people—agents of the chief priests, scribes, and elders in Jerusalem armed with swords and clubs.

⁴⁴The signal they had arranged *was a kiss*. "Watch to see whom I kiss; He's the One," Judas had told them. "Arrest Him, and take Him into secure custody."

⁴⁵As soon as they arrived, Judas stepped forward.

Judas *(kissing Jesus)*	My Teacher.*

⁴⁶*Immediately,* the soldiers grabbed Jesus and took Him into custody.

⁴⁷Now one *of the disciples* standing close by drew his sword and swung, cutting off the ear of a slave of *Caiaphas,* the high priest.

Jesus *(calling out)*	⁴⁸Am I a thief or a bandit that you have to come armed with swords and clubs to capture Me? ⁴⁹I sat teaching in the temple every day with you. You could have taken Me at any time, but you never did. Let the Scriptures be fulfilled; *it will be as it was predicted.*

⁵⁰*When they saw the armed crowd take Jesus into custody,* the disciples fled. ⁵¹One of those following Jesus was a young man who was wearing nothing but a linen cloth. When people from the mob grabbed for him, ⁵²*he wriggled out of their grasp,* left them holding the cloth, and ran naked *into the night.*

⁵³They led Jesus off to see the high priest, *who had gathered a council of religious and civic leaders*, scribes, chief priests, and elders *to hear the evidence and render some decision regarding Jesus.* ⁵⁴Peter followed, at a safe distance, all the way into the courtyard of the high

---

14:45 Literally, Rabbi

priest; and he sat down with the guards to warm himself at their fire. *He hoped no one would notice.*

⁵⁵The chief priests and other religious leaders called for witnesses against Jesus so they could execute Him, but things didn't turn out the way they had planned. ⁵⁶There were plenty of people willing to get up and accuse Jesus falsely, *distorting what Jesus had said or done;* but their testimonies disagreed with each other, *and the leaders were left with nothing.* ⁵⁷Some gave the following distorted testimony.

> **Witnesses** | ⁵⁸We heard Him say, "I will destroy this temple that has been made by human hands; and in three days, I will build another that is not made by human hands."

⁵⁹But even here the witnesses could not agree on exactly what He had said.

⁶⁰The high priest stood up and turned to Jesus.

> **High Priest** | Do You have anything to say *in Your own defense?* What do You think of what all these people have said about You?

⁶¹But Jesus *held His peace and* didn't say a word.

*T*he Liberator had come not as a conquering king but as a sacrificial lamb who would die without defending Himself.

He was accused of setting Himself in the place of God, but He was innocent of that accusation because He is God. But He does not defend Himself because His death protects from punishment the

> sinners who have made themselves like God, ever since Adam ate the fruit in the garden—every single one of us.

High Priest | Are You the Liberating King, the Son of the Blessed One?

Jesus | 62I am. *One day* you will see the Son of Man "sitting at His right hand, *in the place of honor and* power,"* and "coming in the clouds of heaven."*

63Then the high priest, *hearing Jesus quote the Scriptures supporting His authority*, tore his clothes.

High Priest | What else do we need to hear? 64You have heard the
(to the council) | blasphemy from His own lips. What do you have to say about that?

The verdict was unanimous—Jesus was guilty of a capital crime.
65*So the people began to humiliate Him.* Some even spat upon Him. Then He was blindfolded, and they slapped and punched Him.

People | *Come on, Prophet,* prophesy for us! *Tell us who just hit You.*

Then the guards took Him, beating Him as they did so.
66-67While Peter was waiting by the fire outside, one of the servant girls of the high priest saw him.

14:62 Psalm 110:1
14:62 Daniel 7:13

Servant Girl | You were one of those men with Jesus of Nazareth.

Peter | ⁶⁸Woman, I don't know what you're talking about.

He left the fire, and as he went out into the gateway, [a cock crowed.]*
⁶⁹The servant girl saw him again.

Servant Girl | Hey, this is one of them. *One of those who followed Jesus.*

Peter | ⁷⁰No, I'm not one of them.

A little later, some of the other bystanders turned to Peter.

Bystander | Surely you're one of them. You're a Galilean. [We can tell by your accent.]*

⁷¹And then he swore an oath that if he wasn't telling the truth that he would be cursed.

Peter | *Listen,* I don't even know the man you're talking about.

⁷²And as he said this, a cock crowed [a second time]*; and Peter remembered what Jesus had told him: "Before the cock crows [twice]*, you will have denied Me three times."
   He began to weep.

14:68 Some of the early manuscripts omit this portion.
14:70 Some of the early manuscripts omit this portion.
14:72 Some of the early manuscripts omit this portion.
14:72 Some of the early manuscripts omit "twice."

Mark 15

ACCESS TO GOD

¹When morning came, the chief priests met in council with all the Jewish leaders. They bound Jesus, led Him away, and turned Him over to *the Roman governor,* Pilate.

Pilate
(after hearing them) | ²Are You the King of the Jews?

Jesus | You have said so.

³The chief priests went on to accuse Jesus of many things, but Jesus simply stood quietly.

Pilate | ⁴Do You have anything to say? How do You respond to all these charges that have been made against You?

⁵But Jesus said nothing more, and Pilate was astonished.
⁶Now it was his custom at that feast that Pilate should release one prisoner from custody, whomever the people most desired. ⁷There was one rebel from those imprisoned for insurrection *against the Roman occupation.* He had committed murder during an uprising. His name was Barabbas. ⁸A crowd had gathered *in front of Pilate's judgment seat* to request that Pilate follow his usual custom.
⁹Pilate turned to them.

Pilate | Why don't I release to you the King of the Jews?

¹⁰He knew that the chief priests had delivered Jesus because they were threatened by Him, *not because Jesus was a criminal.*

¹¹But priests moved among the crowd and persuaded them to call for Barabbas instead.

> **Pilate** | ¹²Then what do you want me to do with the King of the Jews?

> **Crowd** | ¹³Crucify Him, *crucify Him!*

*C*rucifixion was a painful method of capital punishment often used by the Romans to publicly humiliate and make an example of rabble-rousers, and Pilate had sentenced many to die on Roman crosses.

¹⁴But now he called to them.

> **Pilate** | Why? What has He done to deserve such a sentence?

> **Crowd** | Crucify Him, *crucify Him!*
> *(crying all the*
> *louder)*

*B*arabbas was active and militant, a Jewish leader against the Roman occupiers. In one sense, the choice that the crowd was offered—to have either Jesus or Barabbas released—could be seen as a choice between two types of revolutions. Did they want a revolution of power, a revolution that was easily visible, a revolution that would conquer their enemies in a way they could understand? Or did they want a revolution of healing, a revolution of love, a revolution that brought the kingdom of God to earth in a mystical, transcendental, no less real way? In the heat of the moment, it's no wonder they made the choice they did. Who wants a gentle revolution in a time of war?

[15]When Pilate saw that he could not persuade the crowd to change its mind, he released Barabbas to them and had Jesus publicly whipped, *which was the normal prelude to crucifixion.* Then he had Jesus led away to be crucified. [16]The soldiers took Him into the headquarters of the governor; and the rest of the soldiers in the detachment gathered there, *hundreds of them.* [17]They put a purple robe on Him, and made a crown of thorns that they forced onto His head, [18]and they began to cry out in mock salute.

Soldiers | Hail to the King of the Jews!

[19]For a long while they beat Him on the head with a reed, spat upon Him, and knelt down *as if to honor Him.* [20]When they had finished mocking Him, they stripped off His purple robe and put His own clothes back on Him. Then they took Him away to be executed.

[21]Along the way, they met a man from Cyrene, Simon (the father of Rufus and Alexander), who was coming in from the fields; and they ordered him to carry *the heavy crossbar of* the cross. [22]And so they came at last to *the execution site,* a hill called Golgotha, which means the "Place of a Skull."

²³The soldiers offered Jesus wine mixed with myrrh *to dull His pain,* but He refused it. ²⁴And so they crucified Him, divided up His clothes, and cast lots *(an ancient equivalent of rolling dice)* to see who would keep the clothes *they had stripped from Him.*

²⁵His crucifixion began about nine o'clock in the morning. ²⁶Over His head hung a sign that indicated the charge for which He was being crucified. It read, "THE KING OF THE JEWS." ²⁷On either side of Him were two insurgents *who also had received the death penalty.* ²⁸[And the Hebrew Scripture was completed that said, "He was considered *just another* criminal."]*

²⁹Those passing by on their way into or out of Jerusalem insulted and ridiculed Him.

Some in the Crowd	So You're the One who was going to destroy the temple and rebuild it in three days? ³⁰*Well, if You're so powerful,* then why don't You rescue Yourself? Come on down from the cross!

Chief Priests and Scribes *(mocking Jesus among themselves)*	³¹He rescued others, but He can't rescue Himself. ³²Let the Liberator—the King of Israel—come down from the cross now, and we will see it and believe.

Even the insurgents who were being crucified next to Him taunted Him and reviled Him.

³³At noon, the day suddenly darkened for three hours across the entire land. ³⁴Sometime around three o'clock Jesus called out in a loud voice.

15:28 Some manuscripts omit verse 28, a quote from Isaiah 53:12.

Jesus | Eloi, Eloi, lama sabachthani?

Jesus was speaking, as in the Psalms, "My God, My God, why have You turned Your back on Me?"*
³⁵Some of those standing nearby misunderstood Him.

Bystanders | Hey, He's calling for Elijah.

Many Jews believed that Elijah would return someday. ³⁶One of them filled a sponge with wine that had turned to vinegar and lifted it to Jesus' lips on a stick so He could drink.

Bystander | Let's see if Elijah will come to take Him down.

³⁷Then Jesus cried out with a loud voice, and He took His last breath.
³⁸*At that moment,* the curtain in the temple *that separated the most holy place from the rest of the temple* was torn in two from top to bottom.

*T*he tearing of the temple veil was tremendously significant as a sign of what Jesus' death had accomplished. The heart of the temple sanctuary was divided into two sections: the holy place and the most holy place. The most holy place was a chamber so sanctified that only the high priest could enter—and then only once a year. There God's presence lived on earth.

A long curtain or veil divided the two areas. The veil allowed access to God, and in some ways, protected an unholy people from a

---

truly holy God. And so, when the veil in the temple ripped, it signified a complete and utter transformation in the relationship between God and humanity. It meant that impure people could now approach God—because they were protected by a better veil now, the veil of Christ's blood. It meant, too, that God was free to enter again and rule the world He made. Only God Himself could have ripped the curtain in two, opening the way for people to come into His presence.

³⁹The Roman Centurion, *the soldier in charge of the executions,* stood in front of Jesus, [heard His words,]* and saw the manner of His death.

Centurion | Surely this man was the Son of God!

⁴⁰Off in the distance, *away from the crowds,* stood some women *who knew and had followed Jesus,* including Mary Magdalene and Mary the mother of the younger James, Joses, and Salome. ⁴¹These were women who used to care for Him when He was in Galilee, and many other women who had followed Jesus to Jerusalem joined them.

⁴²Evening came. The crucifixion had taken place on preparation day, Friday, before the Jewish Sabbath began *at sundown.* ⁴³Joseph of Arimathea, a member of the ruling council who was also *a believer anxiously* waiting for the kingdom of God, went to Pilate and boldly asked for the body of Jesus.

⁴⁴Pilate could not believe Jesus was already dead; so he sent for the Centurion, ⁴⁵who confirmed it. Then Pilate gave Joseph permission to take the body.

15:39 Some early manuscripts omit this portion.

⁴⁶Joseph had the body wrapped in a linen burial cloth he had purchased and laid Him in a tomb that had been carved out of rock. Then he had a stone rolled over the opening *to seal it*. ⁴⁷Mary Magdalene and Mary the mother of Joses were watching as the body was interred, *so they knew where His resting place was.*

ABSOLUTELY CERTAIN

¹⁻²At the rising of the sun, after the Sabbath on the first day of the week, the two Marys and Salome brought sweet-smelling spices they had purchased to the tomb to anoint the body of Jesus. ³Along the way, they wondered to themselves how they would roll the heavy stone away from the opening. ⁴But when they arrived, *they were filled with wonder and awe; the tomb was open, and* the stone was already rolled away in spite of its weight and size.

⁵Stepping through the opening, they were startled to see a young man in a white robe seated inside and to the right.

Man in White | ⁶Don't be afraid. You came seeking Jesus of Nazareth, the One who was crucified. He is gone. He has risen. See the place where His body was laid. ⁷Go back, and tell Peter and His disciples that He goes before you into Galilee, just as He said. You will see Him there *when you arrive.*

⁸The women went out quickly; and when they were outside the tomb, they ran away trembling and astonished. Along their way, they didn't stop to say anything to anyone because they were too afraid.

*M*ark finishes his Gospel in the same way he begins it— quickly, without commentary or explanation. He also finishes it in a very humble way: it is the lowly women who take center stage in this greatest miracle of Jesus. The heavenly messenger sends the women with a commission to tell the disciples what has happened, making them the first preachers of the resurrection.

[⁹After He rose from the dead early on Sunday,* Jesus appeared first to Mary Magdalene, a woman out of whom He had cast seven demons. ¹⁰She brought this news back to all those who had followed Him and were still mourning and weeping, ¹¹but they refused to believe she had seen Jesus alive.

¹²After that, Jesus appeared in a different form to two of them as they walked through the countryside, ¹³and again the others did not believe it.

¹⁴The eleven did not believe until Jesus appeared to them all as they sat at dinner. He rebuked them for their hard hearts—for their lack of faith—because they had failed to believe those witnesses who had seen Him after He had risen.

Jesus | ¹⁵Go out into the world and share the good news with all of creation. ¹⁶Anyone who believes this good news and is ceremonially washed* will be rescued, but anyone who does not believe it will be condemned. ¹⁷And these signs will follow those who believe: they will be able to cast out demons in My name, speak with new tongues, ¹⁸take up serpents, drink poison without being harmed, and lay their hands on the sick to heal them.

16:9 Literally, "the first day of the week." The new creation was underway.
16:16 Literally, immersed, to show repentance

¹⁹After the Lord Jesus had charged the disciples in this way, He was taken up into heaven and seated at the right hand of God. ²⁰The disciples went out proclaiming the good news; and the risen Lord continued working through them, confirming every word they spoke with the signs He performed through them.]*

[And the women did everything they had been told to do, speaking to Peter and the other disciples. Later, Jesus Himself commissioned the disciples to take this sacred and eternal message of salvation far to the East and the West.]*

*T*he remaining eleven disciples took this command as their life's mission. According to tradition, all but one of them (John) were killed for their refusal to stop proclaiming the truth that Jesus was the Liberating King who had been crucified and who had arisen from the dead.

Perhaps the most compelling piece of evidence for the reality of Jesus' resurrection is the lives of the disciples themselves. They dedicated their lives—and their deaths—to the proclamation of this reality. If they hadn't been absolutely certain of the truth of Jesus' resurrection, then they wouldn't have dedicated their lives to announcing it to the world.

Their lives make up the next chapter in the good news of Jesus, the Liberating King.

16:9-20 are not contained in the earliest manuscripts. However, many manuscripts do contain these verses. It is likely the original Gospel ended in 16:8 or that the original ending was lost.
16:8 The earliest manuscripts end the Gospel in 16:8, excluding the bracketed words. One manuscript concludes with the bracketed words.

Section Two // **Other Products from** the voice

An Excerpt from:

The Last Eyewitness: The Final Week

The Voice of Matthew

The Voice of Luke: Not Even Sandals

The Voice Revealed: The True Story of the Last Eyewitness

The Voice of Acts: The Dust Off Their Feet

The Voice of Hebrews: The Mystery of Melchizedek

The Voice from on High

John 13

¹Before the Passover festival began, Jesus was keenly aware that His hour had come to depart from this world and to return to the Father. From beginning to end, Jesus' days were marked by His love for His people. ²Before Jesus and His disciples gathered for dinner, the adversary filled Judas Iscariot's heart with plans of deceit and betrayal. ³Jesus, knowing that He had come from God and was going away to God, ⁴stood up from dinner and removed His outer garments. He then wrapped Himself in a towel, ⁵poured water in a basin, and began to wash the feet of the disciples, drying them with His towel.

Simon Peter	6	*(as Jesus approaches)* Lord, are You going to wash my feet?
Jesus	7	Peter, you don't realize what I am doing, but you will understand later.
Peter	8	You will not wash my feet, now or ever!

I have to interrupt the story so you can get the whole picture. Can you imagine what it would feel like to have Jesus (the creative force behind the entire cosmos) wash your feet?

Have you ever been in a gathering where a rich and powerful person offers to fill your glass? You are thinking, "I should do this myself. How is it that someone of your stature would be willing to serve me?" But later you find yourself serving those who would view you as rich and powerful in the same ways that you were

Jesus Washing the Disciples' Feet

served. Multiply that experience by thousands, and you will have a small glimpse of this powerful expression.

My life changed that day; there was a new clarity about how I was supposed to live. I saw the world in a totally new way. The dirt, grime, sin, pain, rebellion, and torment around me were no longer an impediment to the spiritual path—it was the path.

Where I saw pain and filth, I found an opportunity to extend God's kingdom through an expression of love, humility, and service. This simple act is a metaphor for the lens that Christ gives us to see the cosmos. He sees the people, the world He created—which He loves—He sees the filth, the corruption in the world that torments us. His mission is to cleanse those whom He loves from the horrors that torment them. This is His redemptive work with feet, families, disease, famine, and our hearts.

So many of you have missed the heart of the gospel and Christ's example. When you see sin exposed in people, you shake your head and think how sad it is. Or worse you look down at these people for their rejection of God, lack of understanding, and poor morals. This is not the way of Christ. When Christ saw disease, He saw the opportunity to heal. Where He saw sin, He saw a chance to forgive and redeem. When He saw dirty feet, He saw a chance to wash them.

What do you see when you wander through the market, along the streets, on the beaches, and through the slums? Are you disgusted? Or do you seize the opportunity to expand God's reign of love in the cosmos? This is what Jesus did. The places we avoid, Jesus seeks. Now I must digress to tell a bit of the story from long before. I remember Him leading our little group of disciples into one of the most wretched places I have ever seen. It was a series of pools where the crippled and diseased would gather in hopes of being healed. The stench was unbearable, and no sane person would march into an area littered with wretched bodies and communicable diseases. We followed Him reluctantly as He approached a crippled man on his mat and said to him, "Are you here in this place hoping to be healed?" The disabled man responded, "Kind Sir, I wait, like all of these people for the waters to stir, but I cannot walk. If I am to be healed by the waters, some-one must carry me into the pool. So, the answer to Your question is yes—but I cannot be healed here unless someone will help me. Without a helping hand, someone else beats me to the water each time it is stirred." So, Jesus said, "Stand up, carry your mat and walk." At the moment Jesus uttered these words a healing energy coursed through the man and returned life to his limbs—he stood and walked for the first time in thirty-eight years (5:6-9).

It was not clear to us whether or not this man deserved this miracle. In fact, many of the disciples were disgusted by his lack of gratefulness and that he implicated Jesus to some of the Jewish authorities for healing him on the Sabbath. But God's grace is not earned; it is a beautiful gift to all of us.

When Jesus washed our feet He made an announcement to all who follow His path that life would not be about comfort, health, prosperity, and selfish pursuit.

I have gotten away from the story that was barely started. Let me back up and start almost from the beginning of the story again.

John 13

Simon Peter	6	*(as Jesus approaches)* Lord, are You going to wash my feet?
Jesus	7	Peter, you don't realize what I am doing, but you will understand later.
Peter	8	You will not wash my feet, now or ever!

Jesus		If I don't wash you, you will have nothing to do with Me.
Peter	9	Then wash me but don't stop with my feet. Cleanse my hands and head as well.
Jesus	10	Listen, anyone who has bathed is clean all over except for the feet. But I tell you this, not all of you are clean.

[11]He knew the one with plans of betraying Him, which is why He said, "not all of you are clean." [12]After washing their feet and picking up His garments, He reclined at the table again.

Jesus		Do you understand what I have done to you?
	13	You call Me Teacher and Lord, and truly, that is
	14	who I am. So, if your Lord and Teacher washes your feet, then you should wash one another's
	15	feet. I am your example; keep doing what I do.
	16	I tell you the truth: an apostle is not greater than the master. Those who are sent are not greater
	17	than the One who sends them. If you know these things, and if you put them into practice,
	18	you will find happiness. I am not speaking about all of you. I know whom I have chosen, but let the Scripture be fulfilled that says, "The very same man who eats My bread with Me, will
	19	stab Me in the back." Assuredly, I tell you these truths before they happen, so that when it all
	20	transpires you will believe that I am. I tell you the truth: anyone who accepts the ones I send accepts Me. In turn, the ones who accept Me, also accept the One who sent Me.

CHAPTER 14

Matthew

HEROD AND JOHN; JESUS FEEDS 5,000

¹At this time, the ruler *of Galilee* was Herod *Antipas*. He began to hear reports about all that Jesus was doing.

²*Like the people of Nazareth,* Herod wondered where Jesus' power came from.

Herod *(to his servants)*	He must be John the Teacher who washed ceremonially,* raised from the dead; thus His power.

> *H*erod was quite concerned with the attention that John the Teacher was receiving, but he didn't want to spend precious political capital killing a reputed holy man. On top of that, Jesus was beginning to create an even greater problem for Herod.

³⁻⁵Herod's brother Philip had married a woman named Herodias, *who eventually married Herod.* John denounced Herod's marriage to her as adulterous. Herod was incensed *(not to mention a little fearful)* and wanted to kill John, but he knew the people considered John a prophet. Instead, he bound John and put him in jail.

⁶⁻⁷*There John sat until* Herod's birthday. On that night, *Salome,* Herodias's daughter *by Philip,* came and danced for her stepfather and all his birthday guests. Herod so enjoyed her dancing that he vowed to give her whatever she wanted.

14:2 Literally, John who immersed, to show repentance

Salome *(after whispering with her mother)*	⁸Bring me the head of John the Teacher and Prophet,* displayed on a platter.

> $\mathcal{T}$his was not what Herod had expected—he'd imagined his step-daughter might ask for a necklace or maybe a slave.

⁹Herod still thought it unwise to kill John, but *because he had made such a show of his promise*—because he had actually sworn an oath and *because the scene was playing out* in front of *the watchful eyes* of so many guests—Herod felt bound *to give his stepdaughter what she wanted.* ¹⁰And so he sent orders to the prison to have John beheaded, ¹¹and there was his head, displayed on a platter, given first to *Salome* and then passed on to her mother.

¹²John's disciples went to the prison, got John's body, and buried him. Then they went to tell Jesus.

¹³When Jesus learned what had happened, He got on a boat and went away to spend some time in a private place. The crowds, of course, followed Jesus, on foot from their cities. ¹⁴*Though Jesus wanted solitude,* when He saw the crowds, He had compassion on them, and He healed the sick *and the lame.* ¹⁵At evening-time, Jesus' disciples came to Him.

Disciples	We're in a fairly remote place, and it is getting late; *the crowds will get hungry for supper.* Send them away so they have time to get back to the village and get something to eat.
Jesus	¹⁶They don't need to go back to the village in order to eat supper. Give them something to eat here.

14:8 Literally, John who immersed, to show repentance

Disciples	[17]*But we don't have enough food.* We only have five rounds *of flatbread* and two fish.
Jesus	[18]Bring the bread and the fish to Me.

So the disciples brought Him the five rounds of flatbread, and the two fish, [19]and Jesus told the people to sit down on the grass. He took the bread and the fish, He looked up to heaven, He gave thanks, and then He broke the bread. Jesus gave the bread to the disciples, and the disciples gave the bread to the people; [20]everyone ate and was satisfied. *When everyone had eaten,* the disciples picked up 12 baskets *of crusts and broken pieces of bread and crumbs. Not only was there enough, but there was an abundance.* [21]There were 5,000 men there, not to mention all the women and children.

[22]Immediately, Jesus made the disciples get into the boat and go on to the other side of the sea while He dismissed the crowd. [23]Then, after the crowd had gone, Jesus went up to a mountaintop alone (*as He had intended from the start*). As evening descended, He stood alone on the mountain, praying. [24]The boat was in the water, some distance from land, buffeted and pushed around by waves and wind.

[25]Deep in the night, *when He had concluded His prayers,* Jesus walked out on the water to His disciples *in their boat.* [26]The disciples saw a figure moving toward them and were terrified.

Disciple	It's a ghost!
Another Disciple	A ghost? What will we do?
Jesus	[27] Be still. It is I. You have nothing to fear.
Peter	[28]Lord, if it is really You, then command me to meet You on the water.

| Jesus | ²⁹*Indeed*, come. |

Peter stepped out of the boat onto the water and began walking toward Jesus. ³⁰But when he remembered how strong the wind was, his courage caught in his throat and he began to sink.

| Peter | Master, save me! |

³¹Immediately, Jesus reached for Peter and caught him.

| Jesus | O you of little faith. Why did you doubt *and dance back and forth between following* Me *and heeding fear*? |

³²Then Jesus and Peter climbed in the boat together, and the wind became still. ³³And the disciples worshiped Him.

| Disciples | Truly You are the Son of God. |

³⁴All together, Jesus and the disciples crossed *to the other side of the sea*. They landed at Gennesaret, *an area famous for its princely gardens*. ³⁵The people of Gennesaret recognized Jesus, and they spread word of His arrival all over the countryside. People brought the sick *and wounded* to Him ³⁶and begged Him for permission to touch the fringes of His robe. Everyone who touched Him was healed.

FOR THOSE WHO LOVE GOD

*W*hat are your assumptions as you begin this amazing docu-
ment? What do you assume about Luke as an author—his motives,
his agenda, his assumptions? Any constructive experience of reading involves an amazing interaction so complex that it's a wonder it
ever works at all. First, there are readers across time and space, each
reading with certain questions, certain assumptions, and a certain
worldview. Then there's an author, located in another specific time
and place, embedded in his own context and worldview. The author
and the readers also come from communities or traditions—groups
of people who share their basic worldview and who teach them to
think, write, read, and respond in certain ways.

In all my years of reading (and writing), I've concluded that we
as readers have the obligation to try to enter the writer's world, to
understand him on his own terms and in his own context, rather
than requiring him to enter ours (something he can't do!). That
means that we need to try to imagine Luke's world. Fortunately, we
have Luke's sequel to this Gospel to help us understand more about
him. (It's called the Acts of the Apostles, and the two documents
shed light on each other.) Tradition tells us that Luke is a physician,
active in the early church in the years around A.D. 60. He travels
widely with the emissary Paul; so he is a sort of cosmopolitan person, multicultural in his sensitivities, understanding both Jewish culture and the broader Greco-Roman culture of the Roman Empire. As

a physician, he is more educated than the average person of his day, but I think you'll be impressed with his ability to relate to common people—and especially his skill as a storyteller. Remember that Luke isn't presenting us with a theological treatise (as good and important as theological treatises may be); he's telling us the story of Jesus, gathered from many eyewitnesses. Based on the intended audience of his book (Theophilus—literally, God lover), we can assume he wants to help people who love God to love Him even more by knowing what He has done through Jesus.

¹⁻³For those who love God, several other people have already written accounts of what God has been bringing to completion among us, using the reports of the original eyewitnesses, those who were there from the start to witness the fulfillment of prophecy. Like those other servants who have recorded the messages, I present to you my carefully researched, orderly account of these new teachings. ⁴I want you to know that you can fully rely on the things you have been taught *about Jesus, God's Anointed One.*

⁵*To understand the life of Jesus, I must first give you some background history, events that occurred when* Herod ruled Judea *for the Roman Empire.* Zacharias was serving as a priest *in the temple in Jerusalem* those days as his fathers had before him. He was a member of the priestly division of Abijah *(a grandson of Aaron who innovated temple practices),* and his wife, Elizabeth, was of the priestly lineage of Aaron, *Moses' brother.* ⁶They were good and just people in God's sight, walking with integrity in the Lord's ways and laws. ⁷Yet they had this sadness. Due to Elizabeth's infertility, they were childless,

and at this time, they were both quite old—*well past normal childbearing years*.

*I*n the time of Jesus, Jewish life was centered in the temple in Jerusalem. The temple was staffed by religious professionals, what we might refer to as "clergy" today, called priests. They were responsible for the temple's activities—which included receiving religious pilgrims and their sacrifices (cattle, sheep, goats, and doves). Animal sacrifices sound strange to us—we often associate them with some kind of extremist cult. But in the ancient world, they were quite common. It may help, in trying to understand animal sacrifices, to remember that the slaughter of animals was a daily experience in the ancient world; it was part of any meal that included meat. So perhaps we should think of the sacrifice of animals as, first and foremost, a special meal. This meal brings together the Jewish family from near and far, seeking to affirm their connection to the one true and living God. Their gift of animals was their contribution to the meal. (The priests, by the way, were authorized to use the meat for the sustenance of their families.)

The presentation of the blood and meat of these sacrifices was accompanied by a number of prescribed rituals, performed by priests wearing prescribed ornamental clothing, according to a prescribed schedule. As the story continues, we see these solemn rituals interrupted in a most unprecedented way.

[8]One day, Zacharias was chosen to perform his priestly duties in God's presence, according to the temple's normal schedule and

routine. ⁹He had been selected from all the priests by the customary procedure of casting lots *for a once-in-a-lifetime opportunity* to enter the sacred precincts of the temple. There he burned sweet incense, ¹⁰while outside a large crowd of people prayed. ¹¹*Suddenly, Zacharias realized he was not alone:* a messenger of the Lord was there with him. The messenger stood just to the right of the altar of incense. ¹²Zacharias was shocked and afraid, ¹³but the messenger reassured him.

Messenger | Zacharias, calm down! Don't be afraid!

*A*gain and again, when people encounter God (or when they receive a message from God, often through a vision of a heavenly messenger), their first response is terror; and so they need to be calmed down before they can receive the message. We might think Zacharias shouldn't be surprised to hear from God; after all, he's a priest working in the temple. But priests didn't normally hear from God. Those who heard from God were called prophets, not priests.

Priests worked "the family business," so to speak. One became a priest by being born in a priestly family line. Prophets, on the other hand, arose unpredictably. Prophets had no special credentials except the message they carried. So Zacharias had no reason to believe his duties would be interrupted in this way.

Often in the biblical story, when people receive a message from God, after getting over the initial shock, they start asking questions. They push back; they doubt. However, when the word of the Lord comes to people, it doesn't turn them into unthinking zombies or robots; it doesn't override their individuality or capacity to think. Perhaps many of us in some way hear the voice of the Lord, but we don't realize it because we're expecting lightning flashes and a voice with a lot of reverb, a voice so overpowering that we are incapable of questioning and doubting it.

Messenger | Zacharias, your prayers have been heard. Your wife is going to have a son, and you will name him John. [14]He will bring you great joy and happiness—and many will share your joy at John's birth.

[15]This son of yours will be a great man in God's sight. He will not drink alcohol in any form; *instead of alcoholic spirits*, he will be filled with the Holy Spirit from the time he is in his mother's womb. [16]*Here is his mission: he will stop many of the children of Israel in their misguided paths, and* he'll turn them around to follow the path to the Lord their God instead.

[17]Do you remember the prophecy about someone to come in the spirit and power of the prophet Elijah; someone who will turn the hearts of the parents back to their children;* someone who will turn the hearts of the disobedient to the mind-set of the just and good? Your son is the one who will fulfill this prophecy: he will be the Lord's forerunner, the one who will prepare the people and make them ready for God.

1:17 Malachi 4:5-6

*W*e mentioned that Luke was a master storyteller, so we've decided to contextualize his method of storytelling to our own culture in some creative ways. First, we'll highlight dialogue (as you'll see we do in this episode), rendering Luke's account in the form of a screenplay. Second, from time to time, we'll have Luke say, "Picture this," or "Imagine this." Then we'll use present tense to help you enter the story imaginatively, as if you were there yourself.

Zacharias | ¹⁸How can I be sure of what you're telling me? I am an old man, and my wife is far past the normal age for women to bear children. *This is hard to believe!*

Messenger | ¹⁹I am Gabriel, the messenger who inhabits God's
(sternly) presence. I was sent here to talk with you and bring you this good news. ²⁰Because you didn't believe my message, you will not be able to talk—not another word—until you experience the fulfillment of my words.

²¹Meanwhile, the crowd at the temple wondered why Zacharias hadn't come out of the sanctuary yet. It wasn't normal for the priest to be delayed so long. ²²When at last he came out, *it was clear from his face something had happened in there.* He was making signs with his hands to give the blessing, but he couldn't speak. They realized he had seen some sort of vision. ²³When his time on duty at the temple came to an end, he went back home to his wife. ²⁴Shortly after his return, Elizabeth became pregnant. She avoided public contact for the next five months.

Elizabeth | ²⁵I have lived with the disgrace of being barren for all these years. Now God has looked on me with favor. When I go out in public *with my baby*, I will not be disgraced any longer.

²⁶Six months later in Nazareth, a city in *the rural province of* Galilee, the heavenly messenger Gabriel made another appearance. This time, the messenger was sent by God ²⁷to meet with a virgin named Mary, who was engaged to a man named Joseph, a descendant of King David himself. ²⁸The messenger entered her home.

Messenger | Greetings! You are favored, and the Lord is with you! [Among all women on the earth you have been blessed.]*

²⁹The heavenly messenger's words baffled Mary, and she wondered what type of greeting this was.

Messenger | ³⁰Mary, don't be afraid. You have found favor with God. ³¹Listen, you are going to become pregnant. You will have a Son, and you must name Him "Liberation," *or* Jesus.* ³²Jesus will become the greatest among men. He will be known as the Son of the Highest God. God will give Him the throne of His ancestor David, ³³and He will reign over the covenant family of Jacob forever.

1:28 The earliest manuscripts omit this portion.
1:31 Through the naming of Jesus, God is speaking prophetically about the role Jesus will play in our salvation.

$\mathcal{M}$y name is John. My father's name was Zebedee. We made our living by fishing on the Sea of Galilee. I am the last eyewitness to the life of Jesus. All the rest are gone; some long gone. Many died years ago, tragically young, the victims of Roman cruelty and persecution. For some reason, Jesus chose me to live to be an old man. In fact, some in my community have taken to calling me "the elder."

I am the inspiration behind the Fourth Gospel. These are my stories, recorded, told to you by my disciples. I'm proud of what they have done. Me? I've never done much writing. But the story is truly mine.

You see my hands. They've been hurting for the past 20 years now. I couldn't hold a pen even if I wanted to. Not that I was ever good at writing. I was a fisherman, so my hands were calloused. I could tie ropes, mend nets, and pull the oars, but never make a decent xi (Greek letter). So we used secretaries when we wanted to write. There was always a bright young man around it seems, ready to take a letter or help us put pen to papyrus.

My eyes are too weak to read anymore. I can't remember the last time I could see well enough to read a letter or even see the inscriptions. So one of the brothers (I call them my "little children") reads to me. They are all very gracious to me in my old age, compiling my stories, bringing me food, laughing at my jokes, and caring for my most intimate needs. Time is taking its toll on me though. I rarely have the energy to tell the old stories and preach entire sermons. Instead, I simply remind them of the Liberating King's most vital command, saying as loudly as I can, "Little children, love one another."

Jesus had this group of guys. He called us "the twelve." We traveled with Him, spent time with Him, ate with Him, and listened to Him talk about God's kingdom. We watched Him perform miracles. These weren't the tricks like you see in the market or attempts at magic you hear about at shrines. These were what I call "signs." Something was breaking into our darkness. These signs pointed to a greater reality most people didn't even know was there. In the other Gospels, they call them "miracles" or "works of power." We've decided to tell you about select signs because these, more than any, revealed the true glory of this man.

Jesus wanted us to be His family, a different kind of community. We figured it out later. By calling us "the twelve," Jesus was remembering the original twelve tribes of Israel while creating a new people of God. God was doing something new, like the prophets had promised. We were living at the center of history. From now on, everything would be different. This made us feel special, proud, and sometimes arrogant. We'd sometimes jockey for Jesus' attention. Even within the twelve some were closer to Jesus. He had this "inner circle" of sorts. I was part of it. Peter, Andrew, James, and I were with Jesus at times when the other fellows had to stay behind. I'm not sure why He picked me. Because of that, I knew He loved me and I would have a special place with Him.

Jesus also had other students. Not all of them stayed. Some came, and some went. I don't really know how many people in all. One time He sent out 70 of us to proclaim the good news and heal in His name. He even let women be His students. Most people don't know this, but women were among those who helped support us financially.[1] At a time when people said it was a shame for a man to be supported by women, Jesus took their help and took it gladly. But there were no women among the twelve. That was only right. In our day, women didn't travel with men who were not family. Scandal was always swirling around Jesus; He didn't want or need to fight that battle.

I've outlived all the rest of the twelve and His other followers. I can't tell you how lonely it is to be the last person

---

[1] Luke 8:3

with a memory, some would even say a fuzzy memory, of what Jesus looked like, the sound of His voice, the manner of His walk, the penetrating look in His eyes. All I can do is tell my story.

Others have written accounts of what happened among us. The other Gospels have faithfully portrayed the public Jesus. But I feel compelled to tell the story of the private Jesus. The others show us how Jesus preached and dealt with the multitudes. But I still remember the small group time with Jesus and the conversations He had with Nicodemus, the Samaritan woman, and the man born blind—I don't remember his name.

The other Gospels tell the tragedy and injustice of Jesus' death. Here was the single greatest man in history who was falsely accused; who was dragged before corrupt priests and a cruel Roman governor. He was condemned to death and crucified in a most hideous manner. On a human level, Jesus' arrest, condemnation, and crucifixion were tragedies of epic proportions. But the more this old man thinks about what happened, the more I understand now that Jesus' death was His greatest hour. Things seemed to spin out of control so quickly. One minute we were celebrating the Passover together in the upper room; the next we were running for our lives! I'm not sure who was to blame for what happened to Jesus. Envious priests? The Roman governor? But, in fact, He was in complete control. That's why I say the hour of His death was the hour of His greatest glory. That's why I think that when Jesus was lifted up on the cross, He became the means by which all people can come to God. The most vivid memory that lingers in this old man's mind is of Jesus up there on the cross. I can still see it like it was yesterday. His body—hanging halfway between heaven and earth, embracing the world—bridged the gap between God and humanity.

Now I want to be very clear. This is my story, but unlike

what you hear from most storytellers, this is completely true. I am giving you the testimony of an eyewitness. And like my brother disciples, I will swear upon my life that it is true.

John 1

¹Before time itself was measured, the Voice was speaking. The Voice was and is God. ²This *celestial* Voice remained ever present with the Creator; ³His speech shaped the entire cosmos. *Immersed in the practice of creating,* all things that exist were birthed in Him. ⁴His breath filled all things with a living, breathing light. ⁵Light that thrives in the depths of darkness, *blazing through murky bottoms.* It cannot, and will not, be quenched.

⁶A man named John, who was sent by God, *was the first to clearly articulate the source of this unquenchable Light.* ⁷This wanderer, *John who ritually cleansed,** put in plain words the *elusive mystery of the Divine* Light that all might believe through him. *Because John spoke with power, many believed in the Light. Others wondered whether he might be the Light,* ⁸but John was not the Light. He merely pointed to the Light; *and in doing so, he invited the entire creation to hear the Voice.*

⁹The true Light, who shines upon the heart of everyone, was coming into the cosmos. ¹⁰*He does not call out from a distant place but draws near.* He enters our world, a world He made *and speaks clearly,* yet His creation did not recognize Him. ¹¹*Though the Voice utters only truth,* His own people, *who have heard the Voice before,* rebuff this inner calling and refuse to listen. ¹²But those who *hear and* trust the beckoning of the Divine Voice and embrace Him, they shall be reborn as children of God, ¹³He bestows this birthright not by human

---

* 1:7 Literally, immersed, to show repentance

power or initiative but by God's will. *Because we are born of this world, we can only be reborn to God by accepting His call.*

[14]The Voice *that had been an enigma in the heavens chose to* become human and live surrounded by His creations. We have seen Him. Undeniable splendor enveloped Him—the one true Son of God—*evidenced in* the perfect balance of grace and truth. [15]John, *the wanderer* who testified of the Voice, introduced Him. "This is the one I've been telling you is coming. He is much greater than I because He existed *long* before me." [16]Through this man we all receive *gifts of* grace beyond our imagination. *He is the Voice of God.* [17]You see, Moses gave us rules to live by, but Jesus the Liberating King offered the gifts of grace and truth *which make life worth living.* [18]God, unseen until now, is revealed in the Voice, God's only Son, *straight from* the Father's heart.

*B*efore Jesus came along, many thought John the Immerser might be the Liberating King. But when Jesus appeared in the wilderness, John pointed us to Him. The Immerser knew his place in God's redemptive plan. John the Immerser was a man sent from God, but Jesus is the Voice of God. John rejected any messianic claim outright. Jesus, though, accepted it with a smile, but only from a few of us—at least at first. Don't get me wrong, John was important, but he wasn't the Liberating King. He preached repentance. He told everybody to get ready for One greater to come along. The One who comes will immerse us in fire and power, he said. John even told some of his followers to leave him and go follow Jesus.

[19]The words of the Immerser were *gaining attention,* and many had questions, including Jewish religious leaders from Jerusalem. [28]Their entourage approached John in Bethany just beyond the Jordan River while he was cleansing[*] followers in water, *and bombarded him with questions:*[*]

---

* 1:28 Literally, immersing, to show repentance
* 1:28 Verse 28 has been inserted here to help retain the continuity of events.

Religious Leaders: Who are you?

John the Immerser: [20]I'm not the Liberator, *if that is what you are asking.*

Religious Leaders: [21]*Your words sound familiar, like a prophet's.* Is that how we should address you? Are you the Prophet Elijah?

John the Immerser: No, I am not Elijah.

Religious Leaders: Are you the Prophet *Moses told us would come?*

John the Immerser: No.

They continued to press John, unsatisfied with the lack of information.

Religious Leaders: [22]Then tell us who you are and what you are about because everyone is asking us, *especially the Pharisees,* and we must prepare an answer.

[23]John replied with the words of Isaiah:

John the Immerser: *Listen!* I am a voice calling out in the wilderness.
   Straighten out the road for the Lord. *He's on His way.*[*]

[24-25]Then, some priests who were sent by the Pharisees started in on him again.

Religious Leaders: How can you *travel the countryside* cleansing[*] people from their sins if you are not the Liberator or Elijah or the Prophet?

John the Immerser: [26]Cleansing[*] with water is what I do, but the One *whom I speak of, whom we all await,* is standing among you and you have no idea who He is. [27]Though He comes after me, I am not even worthy to unlace His sandals.[*]

---

* 1:23 Isaiah 40:3
* 1:24-25 Literally, immersing, to show repentance
* 1:26 Literally, immersion, to show repentance
* 1:27 Verse 28 has been moved before verse 20 to retain the continuity of events.

Acts 2

A TASTE OF THE KINGDOM

¹When the holy day of Pentecost came *50 days after Passover*, they were gathered together in one place.

Picture yourself among the disciples: ²A sound roars from the sky without warning, the roar of a violent wind, and the whole house where you are gathered reverberates with the sound. ³Then a flame appears, dividing into smaller flames and spreading from one person to the next. ⁴All the apostles are filled with the Holy Spirit and begin speaking in languages they've never spoken, as the Spirit empowers them.

⁵*Because of the holiday,* there were devoted Jews staying as pilgrims in Jerusalem from every nation under the sun. ⁶They heard the sound, and a crowd gathered. They were amazed because each of them could hear the group speaking in their native languages. ⁷They were shocked and amazed by this.

Pilgrims | Just a minute. Aren't all of these people Galileans? ⁸How in the world do we all hear our native languages being spoken? ⁹*Look*—there are Parthians *here*, and Medes, Elamites, Mesopotamians, and Judeans, residents of Cappadocia, Pontus, and Asia, ¹⁰Phrygians and Pamphylians, Egyptians and Libyans from Cyrene, Romans including both Jews by birth and converts, ¹¹Cretans, and Arabs. We're each, in our own languages, hearing these people talk about God's powerful deeds.

¹²Their amazement became confusion as they wondered,

Pilgrims | What does this mean?

Skeptics | ¹³It doesn't mean anything. They're all drunk on some fresh wine!

*N*o matter who you were or what you may have seen, this miraculous sign of God's kingdom would have astounded you. The followers of Jesus were not known as people who drank too much wine with breakfast, but this unusual episode required some kind of explanation. Unfortunately, we can't comprehend or express what transpired on Pentecost. But this was not a novelty performance; rather, it was a taste of the kingdom of God.

¹⁴As the twelve stood together, Peter shouted to the crowd,

Peter | Men of Judea and all who are staying here in Jerusalem, listen. I want you to understand: ¹⁵these people aren't drunk as you may think. Look, it's only nine o'clock in the morning! ¹⁶*No, this isn't drunkenness; this is the fulfillment of the prophecy of Joel. ¹⁷Hear what God says!*

> In the last days, I will offer My Spirit to humanity as a libation.
> Your children will boldly speak *the word of the Lord.*

Young warriors will see visions, and your elders will
dream dreams.

[18]Yes, in those days I shall offer My Spirit to all servants,
Both male and female [and they will boldly speak the
word of the Lord].

[19]And in the heaven above and on the earth below,
I shall give signs *of impending judgment*: blood, fire, and
clouds of smoke

[20]The sun will become a void of darkness, and the moon
will become blood.

Then the great and dreadful day of the Lord will arrive,

[21]And everyone who pleads using the name of the Lord
Will be liberated *into God's freedom and peace*.*

[22]All of you Israelites, listen to my message: it's about
Jesus of Nazareth, a Man whom God authenticated for
you by performing in your presence powerful deeds,
wonders, and signs through Him, just as you yourselves
know. [23]This *Man, Jesus*, who came into your hands by
God's sure plan and advanced knowledge, you nailed to
a cross and killed in collaboration with lawless Gentiles.
[24]But God raised Jesus and unleashed Him from the ago-
nizing birth-pains of death, for death could not possibly
keep Jesus in its power. [25]David spoke *of Jesus'
resurrection*, saying:

The Lord is ever present with me. I will not live in
fear or abandon my calling because He guides my

---

right hand. [26]My heart is glad; my soul rejoices; my body is safe. Who could want for more? [27]You will not abandon me to experience the suffering of a miserable afterlife. Nor leave me to rot alone. [28]Instead, You direct me on a path that leads to a beautiful life. As I walk with You the pleasures are never-ending, and I know true joy and contentment.*

[29] My fellow Israelites, I can say without question that David our ancestor died and was buried, and his tomb is with us today. [30]*David wasn't speaking of himself; he was speaking as a prophet. He saw with prophetic insight* that God had made a solemn promise to him: God would put one of his descendants on His throne. [31]Here's what David was seeing in advance; here's what David was talking about—the Messiah, the Liberating King, would be resurrected. *Think of David's words about* Him not being abandoned to the place of the dead nor being left to decay in the grave. [32]*He was talking about* Jesus, the One God has raised, whom all of us have seen with our own eyes and announce to you today. [33]Since Jesus has been lifted to the right hand of God—*the highest place of authority and power*—and since Jesus has received the promise of the Holy Spirit from the Father, He has now poured out what you have seen and heard here today. [34]*Remember:* David couldn't have been speaking of himself rising to the heavens when he said, "The Lord God said to my Lord, the King,

---

2:28 Psalm 16:8-11

³⁵"Sit here at My right hand, in the place of honor and power, and I will gather Your enemies together, lead them in on hands and knees, and You will rest Your feet on their backs.'"*

³⁶Everyone in Israel should now realize with certainty *what God has done*: God has made Jesus both Lord and Liberating King—this same Jesus whom you crucified.

³⁷When the people heard this, their hearts were pierced and they said to Peter and his fellow apostles,

Pilgrims | Our brothers, what should we do?

Peter | ³⁸Reconsider your lives; change your direction. Participate in the ceremonial washing* in the name of Jesus the Liberating King. Then your sins will be forgiven, and the gift of the Holy Spirit will be yours. ³⁹For the promise *of the Spirit* is for you, for your children, for all people—even those considered outsiders and outcasts—the Lord our God invites everyone to come to Him. Let God liberate you from this decaying culture!

Peter was pleading and offering many logical reasons to believe. ⁴¹Whoever made a place for his message in their hearts received the ceremonial washing*; in fact, that day alone, about 3,000 people joined the disciples.

2:35 Psalm 110:1
2:38 Literally, immersion, a rite of initiation and purification
2:41 Literally, immersion, a rite of initiation and purification

⁴²The community continually committed themselves to learning what the apostles taught them, gathering for fellowship, breaking the bread, and praying. ⁴³Everyone felt a sense of awe because the apostles were doing many signs and wonders among them. ⁴⁴There was an intense sense of togetherness among all who believed; they shared all their material possessions in trust. ⁴⁵They sold any possessions and goods *that did not benefit the community* and used the money to help everyone in need. ⁴⁶They were unified as they worshiped at the temple day after day. In homes, they broke bread and shared meals with glad and generous hearts. ⁴⁷The new disciples praised God, and they enjoyed the goodwill of all the people of the city. Day after day the Lord added to their number everyone who was experiencing liberation.

*A*lthough this young and thriving church had no political influence, property, fame, or wealth, it was powerful. Its power was centered in living the gospel. The people valued one another more than any possessions. They came together as a large, passionate, healthy family where it was natural to pray and share all of life together. The kingdom of God was blossoming on earth as these lovers of God embraced the teachings of Christ. The church has since lost much of the beauty and appeal we see in Acts. It has become concerned with a desire for material possessions, cultural influence, and large congregations.

SURROUNDED BY WITNESSES

*W*e are not alone. We may feel like we are the only ones, but we aren't. We are surrounded by a cloud of martyrs, an army of witnesses. They have run the race of faith and finished well. They have passed the baton to us. It is now our turn. They are pulling for us, praying for us, cheering us on. But how will we run? Will we run our own race or try to run somebody else's? Will our pace be slackened by the weight of guilt and sin? Will we grow tired and give up before the end? Before we know it, we'll pass the baton of faith and take our place in the stands with the witnesses.

¹So since we stand surrounded by *all those who have gone before,* an enormous cloud of witnesses, let us drop every extra weight, every sin that clings to us *and slackens our pace,* and let us run with endurance the long race set before us. ²Now stay focused on Jesus, who designed and perfected our faith. He endured the cross and ignored the shame *of that death* because He focused on the joy that was set before Him; and now He is seated beside God on the throne, *a place of honor.*

³Consider *the life of* the One who endured such *personal attacks and* hostility from sinners so that you will not grow weary or lose heart. ⁴Among you, in your striving against sin, none has resisted *the pressure* to the point of death, as He did.

*G*od *disciplines* His *disciples*. The words look so similar because at the heart of both is "training." Life—with all its hardships and hostilities—is God's training ground for those who belong to Him. What is He training us for? Ironically, He's training us for life—to live and to live well. Not just to live here and now, but to have life in the age to come. He's training us to share His life and holiness. He's training us so that we might finish the race of faith with strength and endurance. He's training us so that our lives might be instruments of peace and justice.

⁵Indeed, you seem to have forgotten the proverb directed to you as children:

My child, do not ignore the instruction that comes from the
> Lord,
> or lose heart when He steps in to correct you;
⁶For the Lord disciplines those He loves,
> and He corrects each one He takes as His own.*

⁷Endure hardship as God's discipline *and rejoice* that He is treating you as His children, for what child doesn't experience discipline from a parent? ⁸But if you are not experiencing the correction that all true children receive, then it may be that you are not His children after all. ⁹Remember, when our human parents disciplined us, we respected them. *If that was true,* shouldn't we respect and live un-

---

12:5-6 Proverbs 3:11-12

der the correction of the Father of all spirits even more? ¹⁰Our parents corrected us for a time as seemed good to them, but God only corrects us to our good so that we may share in His holiness.

¹¹*I'll admit it:* when punishment is happening, it never seems pleasant, only painful. Later, though, it yields the peaceful fruit called righteousness to everyone who has been trained by it. ¹²So lift up your hands that are dangling and brace your weakened knees. ¹³Make straight paths for your feet so that what is lame *in you* won't be put out of joint, but will heal.

¹⁴Pursue peace with everyone, and holiness, since no one will see God without it. ¹⁵Watch carefully that no one falls short of God's favor, that no well of bitterness springs up to trouble you and throw many others off the path ¹⁶Watch that no one becomes wicked and vile like Esau, *the son of Isaac,* who for a single meal sold his invaluable birthright. ¹⁷You know *from the stories of the patriarchs* that later, when he wished to claim his blessing, he was turned away. He could not reverse his action even though he shed bitter tears over it.

*T*he Bible is a brutally honest book. It contains stories of liars, murderers, and adulterers; and these are the good guys. If we read the Bible looking only for positive role models, we'll be quickly disappointed. But if we are honest with ourselves and confess our own faults, we will find in Scripture, particularly in the First Testament, that we have much in common with many broken saints of the past. But we must not stay broken. We must follow their path to transformation through repentance and faith. Repentance means a change of heart, a change of mind, and ultimately a change of how we live.

Repentance is not something we can accomplish on our own. God's grace comes to us and enables us to turn away from our sin and to turn back to Him. Some, like Esau, never find their way back. He stands as a perpetual warning to those who refuse to turn back to God. Remember the warning of Jesus: "if you do not consider God's ways and truly change, then friends, you should prepare to face His judgment and eternal death."*

¹⁸You have not come to the place that can be touched *(as Israel did at Mount Sinai), to a mountain crowned* with blazing fire, darkness, gloom, and a windstorm, ¹⁹or to the blast of a trumpet and the sound of a voice—a voice and message so harsh that the people begged not to hear another word. ²⁰(They could not bear the command that was given: that if even a beast touches the mountain, it must be stoned. ²¹The sight was so terrible that even Moses said, "I am trembling with fear."*)

²²No, instead you have come to Mount Zion, to the city of the living God, to the heavenly Jerusalem, to heavenly messengers unnumbered, *to a joyful feast,* ²³to the assembly of the firstborn registered as heaven's citizens, to God the righteous Judge of all, and to the spirits of all the righteous who have been perfected. ²⁴You have come to Jesus, the Mediator of a new covenant *between God and humanity*, and to His sprinkled blood, which speaks a greater word than the blood of Abel *crying out from the earth*.

²⁵See that you don't turn away from the One who is speaking; for

---

Luke 13:3
12:20-21 Exodus 19:12-13; Deuteronomy 9:19

if the ones who heard and refused the One who spoke on earth faced punishment, then how much more will we suffer if we turn away from the One speaking from heaven—[26]the One whose voice in earlier times shook the earth now makes another promise: "Yet once more I will shake not only the earth, but also the heavens"?* [27]The phrase, "Yet once more," means that those things that can be shaken will be removed and taken away, namely, the *first* creation. As a result, what remains will be those things that cannot be shaken. [28]Therefore, let us all be thankful that we are a part of an unshakeable Kingdom and offer to God worship that pleases Him and reflects the awe and reverence we have toward Him [29]for He is like a fierce fire that consumes everything.*

12:26 Haggai 2:6, 21
12:29 Deuteronomy 4:24

The Orchestra Waits with Anticipation (He Will Feed His Fold)

*I*t is midnight. A deep silence blankets the earth. Stars pierce the darkness. A flock of sheep huddle together in a nearby field. A shepherd sits on a rock not far away, fighting sleep but maintaining a watchful eye. But one mischievous young lamb has strayed and lies asleep behind a rock on a nearby hill.

There's a frightful noise. The lamb awakens to the low growl of a wolf coming from the other side of the rock. The lamb cannot move—it is paralyzed with fear. The wolf shrieks; then there's silence. The lamb hooks his neck nervously around the rock, and standing there is the shepherd, its protector, who has killed the wolf and saved the lamb's life.

We are that mischievous lamb, and the Lord is our shepherd. He guides us through the meadows of life and protects us from the dangers that lurk at night. And, as long as we are not too far away from Him, He can clamp down on the snapping jaws of evil.

When Jesus calls Himself "the good shepherd," His disciples hear the echo of Psalm 23, "The Eternal One is my shepherd. . . ." But despite our romantic notions to the contrary, shepherding was not a noble profession in those days. So why would God choose to reveal Himself as a shepherd? It is because we are more like sheep than we'd like to admit and because He has committed Himself to serve, protect, and provide for us.

> I am the good shepherd. The good shepherd lays down His life for the sheep *in His care.* The hired hand is not like the shepherd caring for His own sheep. When a wolf attacks,

snatching and scattering the sheep, he runs for his life, leaving them *defenseless*. The hired hand runs because he works only for wages and does not care for the sheep. I am the good shepherd; I know My sheep, and My sheep know Me. As the Father knows Me, I know the Father; I will give My life for the sheep.[6]

Just as a true shepherd knows each one of his sheep by name, God knows every one of us. And, just as every sheep's life is important to a shepherd, so ours are important to the Good Shepherd.

Isaiah 40:1–3, 11

[1]"Comfort, comfort My people," says your God.
   [2]"With the gentlest words, *tender and kind*,
Assure this city, this site of long-ago chosenness; speak unto Jerusalem
   their battles are over. The terror, the bloodshed, the horror
   of My punishing work is done.
This place has paid for its guilt; iniquity is pardoned;
   its term of incarceration is complete.
   It has endured double the punishment it was due."

[3]A voice is wailing, "In the wilderness,
   get it ready! Prepare the way,
   make it a straight shot. The Eternal One would have it so.
Straighten the way in the wandering desert
   to make the crooked road wide and straight for our God.

[6] John 10:11-15

⁴Where there are steep valleys, treacherous descents, raise the highway,
    lift it up;
    bring down the dizzying heights; humble them.
Fill the potholes and gullies, the rough places.
    Iron out the shoulders flat and wide.
⁵The Eternal One will be, really be, among us.
    The radiant glory *of the Lord* will be revealed.
    All flesh together will take it in.
    Believe it. None other than God, the Eternal One has spoken."

¹¹He will feed His fold like a shepherd;
    God will assure that we are safe and content.
He will gather together His lambs, *the weak and the wobbly ones*
    into His arms,
    carrying them close to His bosom.
And God tenderly leads those *burdened by care-taking*
    Like a shepherd leads the mothers of her lambs.

A recurring theme throughout Scripture is the ideal image that God relates to His people as a shepherd to his sheep. After the conquest of Jerusalem by the Babylonians, prophets and poets described God as the ultimate shepherd—guarding, providing, protecting, leading, and eventually herding His flock back to a New Jerusalem.

But the shepherd image can cut both ways. Israel and Judah often suffered exploitation and harm at the hands of wayward shepherds, harsh leaders more concerned about themselves than about their flock. But in Israel's critical moments, God's prophets envisioned another shepherd striding forward, Jesus our Liberating King. He would do more than shepherd us during this life; He would shepherd us for all the ages to come. And where would David's Son learn to shepherd us? From His Father and our God. The Lord is our shepherd.

Ezekiel 34:11-24

11 This is what the Lord, the Eternal One, says:

Eternal One

I will personally go out searching for My sheep. I will find them wherever they are, *and I will look after them.* 12 In the same way that a shepherd seeks after, *cares for, and watches over* his scattered flock, so will I be the guardian of My congregation. I will be their Rescuer! *No matter where they have scattered, I will journey to find them.* I will bring them back from the places where they were scattered on that dark and cloudy day. *I will reach into hard-to-reach places; I will search out every secret pocket of the earth in order to save them from the darkness.* 13-14 I will call them out from the nations and gather them from the countries, and I will bring them into their own land. I will give them *a sanctuary—a place where they can rest—*in the high mountain pastures and meadows of Israel. The mountain heights of Israel will be their nourishment, *their sanctuary.* I will introduce them to blooming pastures, where they can graze upon rich mountain lands *to* soothe their hunger. I will lead them along the banks of *glistening mountain* streams, *where they can drink clear, pure water and quench their thirst.*

¹⁵I will *watch over My sheep and* feed My flock. *Whenever they are tired*, they can lie down in the cool, *mountain grass* and rest *for as long as they like*. ¹⁶When they are lost, I will look for them and bring back every last stray. I will bind up the injured and strengthen the weak. However, I will make sure the fat and powerful *do not take advantage of the others*. I will feed them a healthy portion of judgment.

¹⁷As for you, my flock, this is what the Lord, the Eternal One says:

Eternal One Watch carefully! I will judge between one sheep and another, between rams and goats. ¹⁸Are you not satisfied grazing in *blooming* pastures, *by feasting off rich mountain lands*? Do you have to trample all of the pastures with your feet? Are you not satisfied drinking out of clear, *pure, mountain* streams? Do you have to muddy all of the *mountain* streams with your feet? ¹⁹Why should the rest of My flock have to graze in trampled pastures and drink from muddied streams because of your *careless* feet?

²⁰Therefore, this is what the Lord, the Eternal One, says:

Eternal One Watch carefully! I will personally judge between the fat sheep and the skinny sheep. ²¹Because you bully the weak and push them around with your haunches, shoulders, and horns until they are scattered all over *the mountains*, ²²I will step in and save them. *I will be their rescuer!* They will no longer be hunted and hassled. I will judge between one sheep and another. ²³I will designate one shepherd over the entire flock: My *faithful* servant,

David. He will *watch over them and* take care of them. He will be their shepherd. ²⁴I, the Eternal One, will be their True God; and My *faithful* servant, David, will be their prince. I, the Eternal One, have spoken.

One of the primary functions of the shepherd is herding. A shepherd shows his concern for the well-being of his flock by keeping them all together, regardless of each animal's whims, and moving them from pasture to pasture safely. The "shepherds" in sixth-century B.C. Jerusalem did not care about the people they led. As a result, most of God's covenant people were scattered among the pagan nations. When God spoke, those attuned to His voice heard His displeasure. They spoke His message, words of rebuke and words of hope. The Eternal One promised to become personally involved: He would bring the miserable shepherds to a miserable end, gather His chosen ones from the nations, and raise up new shepherds to lead His people. Of all the shepherds God promised, there was one Good Shepherd who would overshadow them all. The time was near, the prophets sensed, when the Liberating King, the righteous Branch of David would appear.

Jeremiah 23:1-8

| Eternal One | 1 | Woe to the shepherds who slaughter and scatter My sheep! |

²This is what the Eternal One, the True God of Israel, has to say about the shepherds tending My people:

Eternal One   You have scattered My flock, driven them far away, and failed *miserably* at being their caregivers. *In short, you've been careless, wicked leaders*; therefore, I will punish you for *your negligence*, your careless evil. ³I will personally gather the remnant of My sheep from the lands where I have driven them. I will bring them back to their home-pasture where they will be fruitful and multiply. ⁴I will appoint *new, responsible* shepherds to take care of them, and My sheep will no longer be afraid of anything. *These new, responsible shepherds will watch over every single one of My sheep and will not allow any of them* to go missing.

5   Behold! The time is near
        when I will raise up an *authentic*, righteous Branch
            of David,
        an heir of his royal line,
    A King who will rule justly and act wisely
    And bring righteousness to the land.
6   During His reign, Judah will be redeemed
        and Israel will be a safe place again.
    His name will tell the story:
        the Eternal One, our righteousness!

7   So *be ready and* watch carefully. The time is approaching, coming ever so close when no one will say any longer, "As the Eternal One lives, who freed the Israelites out of slavery in Egypt." ⁸Instead, they will say, "As the Eternal One lives, who *ended our exile* and gathered the descendants of Israel out of the north and out of all other countries where He had scattered them." Then the Israelites will live in their own land.